501 MUST-DRINK COCKTAILS

CONTENTS

INTRODUCTION

Cocktails, whether served at a dedicated cocktail party or as a precursor to an elegant meal, lend an air of sophistication and glamour. There are hundreds and hundreds of different cocktails, some of which experience fleeting popularity before disappearing into obscurity while others remain popular for decades. In *501 Must-Drink Cocktails*, the timeless favourites are collected together with more recent and modern classics.

But what exactly is a cocktail? Traditionally, they are mixed drinks, consisting of one or more spirits, together with flavourings such as fruit, fruit juice, liqueur, syrup, herbs or spices. With a few exceptions, such as Flaming Lamborghini, they are chilled, shaken or stirred with ice, and served over ice or in chilled glasses. Long drinks, such as slings, are topped up with mixers, typically tonic water, soda water or cola. Many of them have traditional decorations – such as fruit wedges, swizzle sticks, olives or cocktail cherries – and are served in specific glasses. Good cocktails (except shots and slammers) are drinks to enjoy slowly. They look attractive, have a balance of flavours and are appealing to both the eye and the palate

Why 'cocktail'?

There are dozens of different possible sources for the word, including *coquetier*, a French egg-cup in which the drinks were served in a New Orleans bar in the early 19th century; a mixed-breed horse called a cock-tail; *decocta*, Latin for distilled; a cock's tail, either that worn by George Washington in his hat or by officers in a particular regiment or one put into drinks to indicate that they contained alcohol; the tailings (dregs) at the bottom of a cask that were drained out through the cock (tap), mixed up and sold cheaply; and 'cock's ale', an ale served at cock fights and in which a sack of half-cooked chicken and other ingredients had been fermented for several days.

History

Flavouring spirits probably became popular because they were originally sold with a far higher alcohol content than they are now – up to 135° proof, instead of today's normal maximum of 40° proof – so juice, water, herbs and spices would have helped to disguise the harsh taste. Different regions developed their own particular recipes, such as juleps in the southern states of the USA and a variety of punches in the Caribbean (although the latter probably originated in India).

Although the word cocktail is now used as a blanket term for a wide variety of mixed drinks – slings, sours, punches, martinis, daiquiris and many more – it was originally confined to a small group of drinks. One early reference – from 1806 – describes a cocktail as 'a stimulating liquor composed of spirits of any kind, sugar, water and bitters – it is vulgarly called a bitter sling…'. They appear to have been regarded as a sort of morning pick-me-up, possibly even a hangover cure. *The Bon Vivant's Companion: or How to Mix Drinks* of 1862 described cocktails as a handful of drinks that included bitters among their ingredients. Among the recipes is one for a Martinez, which later became the Martini.

During the second half of the 19th century, cocktail-drinking really took off. Famous drinks that came into being during this period include the Manhattan (which was invented in the 1870s for Winston Churchill's mother, socialite Jennie Jerome) and the Singapore Sling (which was invented in around 1910–15 in the Raffles Hotel in Singapore).

By this time, the prohibition lobby was gaining ground in the United States and in 1920 the manufacture, sale and consumption of alcoholic drinks were forbidden, which simply sent the trade underground and helped to fuel organized crime. In Europe, however, life for the rich was far more liberated and cocktails continued to be enjoyed, often as pre-lunch appetizers and at cocktail parties. After prohibition ended in 1933, Hollywood films gave cocktails a glamorous image. In the 1970s, vodka took over from gin as the most popular spirit for cocktails, which gave rise to a vast array of new drinks. Then, in the 1980s, with the advent of 'happy hour', things changed. The young no longer wanted classic cocktails, but new inventions such as Brain Haemorrhage and Dirty Sanchez. However, the 1988 film *Cocktail* sparked both a craze for 'flair bartending' and a return to the classics, which have, thankfully, never really gone away.

RUM

GAUGUIN

3 MEASURES CRUSHED ICE
2 MEASURES WHITE RUM
2 TEASPOONS PASSION
FRUIT SYRUP
2 TEASPOONS LEMON
JUICE
1 TEASPOON LIME JUICE
COCKTAIL CHERRY, TO
DECORATE

Put the crushed ice, rum, passion fruit syrup and fruit juices into a food processor or blender and blend at low speed for 15 seconds. Strain into a glass straight up and add a cocktail cherry to decorate.

PORT ANTONIO

½ TEASPOON GRENADINE
4–5 ICE CUBES
1 MEASURE LIME JUICE
3 MEASURES WHITE OR
GOLDEN RUM
LIME RIND, TO DECORATE
COCKTAIL CHERRY, TO
DECORATE

Spoon the grenadine into a chilled cocktail glass. Put the ice cubes into a mixing glass. Pour the lime juice and rum over the ice and stir vigorously, then strain into the cocktail glass. Wrap the lime rind around the cherry, impale them on a cocktail stick and use them to decorate the drink.

Right: Port Antonio

APRICOT DAIQUIRI

CRUSHED ICE
1 MEASURE WHITE RUM
1 MEASURE LEMON JUICE
½ MEASURE APRICOT LIQUEUR
OR BRANDY
3 RIPE APRICOTS, SKINNED AND
STONED
APRICOT SLICE, TO DECORATE
COCKTAIL CHERRY, TO
DECORATE
MINT SPRIG, TO DECORATE

Put some crushed ice into a food processor or blender. Add the rum, lemon juice, apricot liqueur or brandy and the apricots and blend for 1 minute or until smooth. Pour into a chilled cocktail glass and decorate with an apricot slice, cocktail cherry and mint sprig.

FROZEN MANGO DAIQUIRI

CRUSHED ICE
½ MANGO, PEELED AND
STONED
1 MEASURE LIME JUICE
2 MEASURES WHITE RUM
1 TEASPOON ICING SUGAR
MANGO SLICES, TO
DECORATE

Put a small scoop of crushed ice into a food processor or blender. Add the mango, lime juice, rum and icing sugar and blend until smooth. Serve in a chilled glass and decorate with mango slices.

Right: Frozen Mango Daiquiri

ST LUCIA

4–5 ICE CUBES
1 MEASURE CURAÇAO
1 MEASURE DRY
VERMOUTH
JUICE OF ½ ORANGE
1 TEASPOON GRENADINE
2 MEASURES WHITE OR
GOLDEN RUM
ORANGE RIND SPIRAL, TO
DECORATE
COCKTAIL CHERRY, TO
DECORATE

Put the ice cubes into a cocktail shaker and pour the Curaçao, vermouth, orange juice, grenadine and rum over the ice. Shake until a frost forms, then pour without straining into a highball glass. Decorate with an orange rind spiral and a cocktail cherry.

Right: St Lucia

FROZEN MANGO AND MINT SPICED DAIQUIRI

CRUSHED ICE
1 MEASURE LIME JUICE
2 TEASPOONS SUGAR SYRUP
2 MEASURES CAPTAIN MORGAN
ORIGINAL SPICED RUM
½ RIPE MANGO, PEELED AND
ROUGHLY CHOPPED
6 MINT LEAVES
MANGO SLICE, TO DECORATE
MINT SPRIG, TO DECORATE

Put some crushed ice into a food processor or blender. Add the lime juice, sugar syrup, rum, mango and mint leaves and blend until smooth. Pour into a large Champagne saucer and decorate with a mango slice and mint sprig.

RUM OLD-FASHIONED

Stir 1 ice cube with the bitters, sugar and water in a heavy-based old-fashioned glass until the sugar has dissolved. Add the white rum, stir and add the remaining ice cubes. Add the dark rum and stir once again. Decorate with a cherry.

3 ICE CUBES
1 DASH ANGOSTURA BITTERS
1 DASH LIME BITTERS
1 TEASPOON CASTER SUGAR
$\frac{1}{2}$ MEASURE WATER
2 MEASURES WHITE RUM
$\frac{1}{2}$ MEASURE DARK RUM
1 CHERRY, TO DECORATE

EL DORADO

Put the ice cubes into a cocktail shaker. Pour the rum, advocaat and crème de cacao over the ice and add the coconut. Shake until a frost forms, then strain into a chilled cocktail glass.

4–5 ICE CUBES
1 MEASURE WHITE RUM
1 MEASURE ADVOCAAT
1 MEASURE CRÈME DE CACAO
2 TEASPOONS GRATED COCONUT

Left: Rum Old-Fashioned

LIMON MOJITO

1 LIME, QUARTERED
2 TEASPOONS SOFT
BROWN SUGAR
8 MINT LEAVES
CRUSHED ICE
2 MEASURES BACARDI
LIMÓN RUM
SODA WATER, TO TOP UP
(OPTIONAL)
LEMON AND LIME SLICES,
TO DECORATE

Muddle the lime quarters, sugar and mint in a highball glass. Fill the glass with crushed ice and add the rum. Stir and top up with soda water, if you like. Decorate with lemon and lime slices and serve with straws.

FROZEN PINEAPPLE DAIQUIRI

CRUSHED ICE
2½ PINEAPPLE SLICES
½ MEASURE LIME JUICE
1 MEASURE WHITE RUM
¼ MEASURE COINTREAU
1 TEASPOON SUGAR SYRUP
PINEAPPLE WEDGE, TO
DECORATE

Put some crushed ice into a food processor or blender. Add the pineapple slices, lime juice, rum, Cointreau and sugar syrup and blend until smooth. Pour into a chilled Margarita glass and decorate with a pineapple wedge.

MAI TAI

Put some ice cubes into a cocktail shaker with the golden rum, Curaçao, orgeat syrup and lime juice and shake well. Strain over crushed ice into an old-fashioned glass, float the Navy rum on top and decorate with lime rind and a mint sprig.

ICE CUBES, PLUS CRUSHED ICE, TO SERVE
2 MEASURES GOLDEN RUM
½ MEASURE ORANGE CURAÇAO
½ MEASURE ORGEAT SYRUP
JUICE OF 1 LIME
2 TEASPOONS WOOD'S NAVY RUM
LIME RIND, TO DECORATE
MINT SPRIG, TO DECORATE

BLACK WIDOW

Put cracked ice into a tall glass. Put the rum, Southern Comfort, lime juice and sugar syrup into a cocktail shaker. Shake lightly. Strain into a chilled cocktail glass and decorate with a lime slice.

4–5 ICE CUBES, CRACKED
2 MEASURES DARK RUM
1 MEASURE SOUTHERN COMFORT
JUICE OF ½ LIME
1 DASH SUGAR SYRUP
LIME SLICE, TO DECORATE

COCONUT DAIQUIRI

4–5 ICE CUBES, CRUSHED
2 MEASURES WHITE RUM
1 MEASURE COCONUT
LIQUEUR
2 MEASURES LIME JUICE
1 TEASPOON GRENADINE
LIME SLICE, TO DECORATE

Put the crushed ice into a cocktail shaker. Pour the rum, coconut liqueur, lime juice and grenadine over the ice and shake until a frost forms. Strain into a cocktail glass and decorate with a lime slice.

THE BOADAS COCKTAIL

1 MEASURE WHITE RUM
1 MEASURE RED DUBONNET
1 MEASURE ORANGE
CURAÇAO
COCKTAIL CHERRIES, TO
DECORATE

Pour the rum, Dubonnet and Curaçao into a mixing glass and stir well. Pout into a small Martini glass and decorate with cocktail cherries impaled on cocktail sticks.

TOBAGO

Put the rum, gin, lime juice and guava syrup into a cocktail shaker and shake well. Pour into a glass over crushed ice.

½ MEASURE LOW-PROOF RUM
½ MEASURE GIN
1 TEASPOON LIME JUICE
1 TEASPOON GUAVA SYRUP
CRUSHED ICE

FLORIDA SKIES

Put some cracked ice into a tall glass. Put the rum and fruit juices into a cocktail shaker. Shake lightly. Strain into the glass and top up with soda water. Decorate with cucumber or lime slices.

CRACKED ICE
1 MEASURE WHITE RUM
¼ MEASURE LIME JUICE
½ MEASURE PINEAPPLE JUICE
SODA WATER, TO TOP UP
CUCUMBER OR LIME SLICES, TO DECORATE

RUM CRUSTA

LIME WEDGE
CASTER SUGAR
ICE CUBES, PLUS CRUSHED ICE, TO SERVE
2 MEASURES DARK RUM
1 MEASURE COINTREAU
2 TEASPOONS MARASCHINO LIQUEUR
2 TEASPOONS LIME JUICE
2 GRAPES, TO DECORATE

Frost the rim of an old-fashioned glass by moistening it with the lime wedge and pressing it into the sugar. Put some ice cubes into a cocktail shaker with the rum, Cointreau, Maraschino liqueur and lime juice and shake well. Strain into an old-fashioned glass filled with crushed ice and decorate with the grapes.

HAVANA ZOMBIE

4–5 ICE CUBES
JUICE OF 1 LIME
5 TABLESPOONS
PINEAPPLE JUICE
1 TEASPOON SUGAR SYRUP
1 MEASURE WHITE RUM
1 MEASURE GOLDEN RUM
1 MEASURE DARK RUM

Put the ice cubes into a mixing glass. Pour the fruit juices, sugar syrup and rums over the ice and stir vigorously. Pour without straining into a tall glass.

Right: Havana Zombie

PINK ANGEL

ICE CUBES
½ MEASURE WHITE RUM
¼ MEASURE ADVOCAAT
¼ MEASURE CHERRY BRANDY
1 EGG WHITE
½ MEASURE DOUBLE CREAM

Put some ice cubes into a cocktail shaker with the rum, advocaat, cherry brandy, egg white and cream and shake well. Strain into a cocktail glass.

WHITE WITCH

8–10 ICE CUBES
1 MEASURE WHITE RUM
½ MEASURE WHITE CRÈME DE CACAO
½ MEASURE COINTREAU
JUICE OF ½ LIME
SODA WATER, TO TOP UP
ORANGE AND LIME SLICES, TO DECORATE

Put half the ice cubes into a cocktail shaker and pour over the rum, crème de cacao, Cointreau and lime juice. Shake and strain over the remaining ice cubes in an old-fashioned glass. Top up with soda water and stir to mix. Decorate with orange and lime slices and serve with straws.

HURRICANE

Put some ice cubes into a cocktail shaker and pour over the rums, passion fruit syrup and lime juice. Shake well. Strain the drink into a cocktail glass and add ice cubes.

ICE CUBES
1 MEASURE WHITE RUM
1 MEASURE GOLDEN RUM
2 TEASPOONS PASSION FRUIT SYRUP
2 TEASPOONS LIME JUICE

BATISTE

Put the ice cubes into a mixing glass. Pour the Grand Marnier and rum over the ice, stir vigorously, then strain into a cocktail glass.

4–5 ICE CUBES
1 MEASURE GRAND MARNIER
2 MEASURES GOLDEN OR DARK RUM

MOJITO

Muddle the mint leaves, lime wedges and sugar in a highball glass. Fill the glass with crushed ice and add the rum. Stir and top up with soda water. Decorate with mint sprigs.

Left: Mojito

8 MINT LEAVES
½ LIME, CUT INTO WEDGES
2 TEASPOONS CANE SUGAR
CRUSHED ICE
2½ MEASURES WHITE RUM
SODA WATER, TO TOP UP
MINT SPRIGS, TO DECORATE

BOLERO

Put some ice cubes into a cocktail shaker and pour over the rum, apple brandy and vermouth. Shake well. Strain into a glass and add ice cubes. Squeeze the zest from the lemon rind twist over the glass and drop it in.

ICE CUBES
1½ MEASURES WHITE RUM
¾ MEASURE APPLE BRANDY
SEVERAL DROPS SWEET VERMOUTH
LEMON RIND TWIST, TO DECORATE

COOPER COOLER

3–4 ICE CUBES
2 MEASURES GOLDEN RUM
3 MEASURES DRY GINGER ALE
1 TABLESPOON LIME OR LEMON JUICE
LIME OR LEMON SLICE, TO DECORATE

Put the ice cubes into a highball glass. Pour over the rum, ginger ale and lime or lemon juice and stir. Decorate with a lime or lemon slice.

PINK MOJITO

6 MINT LEAVES
½ LIME, CUT INTO WEDGES
2 TEASPOONS SUGAR SYRUP
3 RASPBERRIES
CRUSHED ICE
1½ MEASURES WHITE RUM
½ MEASURE CHAMBORD
CRANBERRY JUICE, TO TOP UP
MINT SPRIG, TO DECORATE

Muddle the mint leaves, lime wedges, sugar syrup and raspberries in a highball glass. Add some crushed ice and the rum and Chambord. Stir well and top up with cranberry juice. Decorate with a mint sprig.

Right: Pink Mojito

BLUE HAWAIIAN

CRUSHED ICE
1 MEASURE WHITE RUM
½ MEASURE BLUE
CURAÇAO
2 MEASURES PINEAPPLE
JUICE
1 MEASURE COCONUT
CREAM
PINEAPPLE WEDGE, TO
DECORATE

Put some crushed ice into a food processor or blender and pour in the rum, Curaçao, pineapple juice and coconut cream. Blend at high speed for 20–30 seconds. Pour into a chilled cocktail glass. Decorate with a pineapple wedge.

PINEAPPLE MOJITO

6 MINT LEAVES
4 PINEAPPLE CHUNKS
2 TEASPOONS SOFT
BROWN SUGAR
2 MEASURES GOLDEN RUM
CRUSHED ICE
PINEAPPLE JUICE, TO TOP
UP
PINEAPPLE WEDGE, TO
DECORATE
MINT SPRIG, TO DECORATE

Muddle the mint leaves, pineapple chunks and sugar in a cocktail shaker. Add the rum and shake well. Strain into a highball glass filled with crushed ice, top up with pineapple juice and stir. Decorate with a pineapple wedge and a mint sprig and serve with straws.

Right: Pineapple Mojito

SERENADE

6 ICE CUBES, CRUSHED
1 MEASURE WHITE RUM
½ MEASURE AMARETTO DI SARONNO LIQUEUR
½ MEASURE COCONUT CREAM
2 MEASURES PINEAPPLE JUICE
PINEAPPLE SLICE, TO DECORATE

Put half the ice cubes into a food processor or blender; add the rum, Amaretto di Saronno, coconut cream and pineapple juice and blend for 20 seconds. Pour into a tall glass over the remaining ice cubes. Decorate with a pineapple slice and serve with a straw.

DISCOVERY BAY

4–5 ICE CUBES
3 DROPS ANGOSTURA BITTERS
JUICE OF ½ LIME
1 TEASPOON CURAÇAO OR BLUE CURAÇAO
1 TEASPOON SUGAR SYRUP
3 MEASURES GOLDEN OR DARK RUM
LIME SLICES, TO DECORATE

Put the ice cubes into a cocktail shaker, then shake the bitters over the ice. Pour in the lime juice, Curaçao, sugar syrup and rum and shake until a frost forms. Strain into an old-fashioned glass. Decorate with lime slices.

HAWAIIAN DELUXE

Put some ice cubes into a cocktail shaker with all the other ingredients, except the grenadine. Shake well. Strain into a large hurricane glass. Drizzle the grenadine over the drink and decorate with pineapple and coconut wedges. Serve with long straws.

ICE CUBES
1½ MEASURES COCONUT RUM
½ MEASURE COINTREAU
½ MEASURE AGED RUM
1 MEASURE COCONUT CREAM
2 MEASURES PINEAPPLE JUICE
1 DASH SUGAR SYRUP
1 DASH LEMON JUICE
1 DASH GRENADINE
PINEAPPLE AND COCONUT WEDGES, TO DECORATE

NEW ORLEANS DANDY

Put the ice cubes into a cocktail shaker. Pour the rum, peach brandy and fruit juices over the ice and shake until a frost forms. Strain into a Champagne flute or tall glass and top up with Champagne.

4–5 ICE CUBES
1 MEASURE WHITE RUM
½ MEASURE PEACH BRANDY
1 DASH ORANGE JUICE
1 DASH LIME JUICE
CHAMPAGNE, TO TOP UP

CUBA LIBRE

ICE CUBES
2 MEASURES GOLDEN RUM
JUICE OF ½ LIME
COLA, TO TOP UP
LIME WEDGES, TO
DECORATE

Fill a highball glass with ice cubes, pour over the rum and lime juice and stir to mix. Top up with cola and decorate with lime wedges. Serve with straws.

I misremember who first was cruel enough to nurture the cocktail party into life. But perhaps it would be not too much to say, in fact it would be not enough to say, that it was not worth the trouble.
DOROTHY PARKER

ALMOND CIGAR

Pour the rum, lime cordial and Amaretto di Saronno into a chilled cocktail shaker. Shake and strain into a chilled Martini glass. Decorate with a cinnamon stick and a lime rind twist.

2 MEASURES HAVANA CLUB 3-YEAR-OLD RUM
1 MEASURE LIME CORDIAL
1 MEASURE AMARETTO DI SARONNO LIQUEUR
CINNAMON STICK, TO DECORATE
LIME RIND TWIST, TO DECORATE

HAVANA BEACH

Cut the lime into 4 pieces and put into a food processor or blender with the pineapple juice, rum and sugar. Blend until smooth. Pour into a hurricane glass or large goblet and top up with ginger ale. Decorate with a lime slice.

½ LIME
2 MEASURES PINEAPPLE JUICE
1 MEASURE WHITE RUM
1 TEASPOON SUGAR
DRY GINGER ALE, TO TOP UP
LIME SLICE, TO DECORATE

BANANA DAIQUIRI

Put the cracked ice into a Margarita glass or tall goblet. Put the rum, banana liqueur, banana and lime cordial into a food processor or blender and blend for 30 seconds. Pour into the glass and decorate with the icing sugar and a banana slice.

3 ICE CUBES, CRACKED
2 MEASURES WHITE RUM
½ MEASURE BANANA LIQUEUR
½ SMALL BANANA
½ MEASURE LIME CORDIAL
1 TEASPOON ICING SUGAR, TO DECORATE
BANANA SLICE, TO DECORATE

CLEM THE CUBAN

Muddle the schnapps, mint sprig and lime wedges in a cocktail shaker, then add the rum and a scoop of crushed ice. Shake very briefly and double strain into a shot glass.

1 DASH APPLE SCHNAPPS
1 MINT SPRIG
2 LIME WEDGES
1 MEASURE HAVANA CLUB 3-YEAR-OLD RUM
CRUSHED ICE

Left: Clem the Cuban

RED RUM

SMALL HANDFUL OF
REDCURRANTS
½ MEASURE SLOE GIN
ICE CUBES
2 MEASURES BACARDI
8-YEAR-OLD RUM
½ MEASURE LEMON JUICE
½ MEASURE VANILLA SYRUP
REDCURRANT STRING, TO
DECORATE

Muddle the redcurrants and sloe gin in a cocktail shaker. Add some ice cubes with the remaining ingredients and shake well. Double strain into a chilled Martini glass. Decorate with a redcurrant string.

Right: Red Rum

RUDE JUDE

ICE CUBES
1 MEASURE WHITE RUM
1 DASH STRAWBERRY
PURÉE
1 DASH STRAWBERRY
SYRUP
1 DASH LIME JUICE

Put some ice cubes into a cocktail shaker and pour over the rum, strawberry purée, strawberry syrup and lime juice. Shake well and strain into a shot glass.

KINKY WITCH

ICE CUBES
1 MEASURE HAVANA CLUB 3-YEAR-OLD RUM
1 MEASURE HAVANA CLUB SILVER DRY RUM
½ MEASURE ORANGE CURAÇAO
½ MEASURE CRÈME DE MURE
½ MEASURE ORGEAT SYRUP
2 MEASURES ORANGE JUICE
2 MEASURES GRAPEFRUIT JUICE
2 TEASPOONS OVER-PROOF RUM
GRAPEFRUIT WEDGES, TO DECORATE

Put some ice cubes into a cocktail shaker with the Havana Club rums, Curaçao, crème de mure, orgeat syrup and fruit juices and shake well. Strain into a highball glass filled with ice cubes, float the over-proof rum on top and decorate with grapefruit wedges.

RUM REFASHIONED

1 BROWN SUGAR CUBE
4 DASHES ANGOSTURA
BITTERS
ICE CUBES
2 MEASURES AGED RUM
SUGAR SYRUP, TO TASTE
LIME RIND TWIST, TO
DECORATE

Put the sugar cube into an old-fashioned glass, then splash in the bitters, add 2 ice cubes and stir. Add a quarter of the rum and another 2 ice cubes and stir. Continue building, and stirring, with the rum and ice cubes, adding sugar syrup to taste. Decorate with a lime rind twist.

Work is the curse of the drinking classes.
OSCAR WILDE

HUMMINGBIRD

Put the crushed ice into a cocktail shaker. Pour the rums, Southern Comfort and orange juice over the ice and shake until a frost forms. Strain into a long glass and top up with cola. Decorate with an orange slice and serve with a straw.

> The important thing is the rhythm. Always have rhythm in your shaking. Now a Manhattan you always shake to fox-trot time, a Bronx to two-step time, a dry Martini you always shake to waltz time.
>
> **WILLIAM POWELL, THE THIN MAN**

4–5 ICE CUBES, CRUSHED
1 MEASURE DARK RUM
1 MEASURE LIGHT RUM
1 MEASURE SOUTHERN COMFORT
1 MEASURE ORANGE JUICE
COLA, TO TOP UP
ORANGE SLICE, TO DECORATE

APPLE-SOAKED MOJITO

Muddle the mint leaves, lime wedges and sugar syrup in a cocktail shaker. Add the rum and shake well. Strain into a highball glass filled with crushed ice and top up with apple juice. Decorate with a mint sprig and apple slices.

8 MINT LEAVES, PLUS AN EXTRA SPRIG TO DECORATE
1/2 LIME, CUT INTO WEDGES
2 TEASPOONS SUGAR SYRUP
2 MEASURES GOLDEN RUM
CRUSHED ICE
APPLE JUICE, TO TOP UP
RED APPLE SLICES, TO DECORATE

TIKI TREAT

Put a small scoop of crushed ice into a food processor or blender with all the other ingredients and blend until smooth. Serve in a stemmed hurricane glass with long straws and decorate with mango slices.

Left: Tiki Treat

CRUSHED ICE
½ RIPE MANGO, PEELED AND STONED, PLUS EXTRA SLICES TO DECORATE
3 COCONUT CHUNKS
1 MEASURE COCONUT CREAM
2 MEASURES AGED RUM
1 DASH LEMON JUICE
1 TEASPOON CASTER SUGAR

JOLLY ROGER

Put half the cracked ice into a cocktail shaker with the rum, Galliano, apricot brandy and orange juice and shake well. Strain into a tall glass over the remaining ice. Decorate with the fruit slices.

5 ICE CUBES, CRACKED
1 MEASURE DARK RUM
1 MEASURE GALLIANO
½ MEASURE APRICOT BRANDY
3 MEASURES ORANGE JUICE
APRICOT, ORANGE AND LEMON SLICES, TO DECORATE

STRAWBERRY AND MINT DAIQUIRI

3 STRAWBERRIES, HULLED
1 DASH STRAWBERRY
SYRUP
6 MINT LEAVES, PLUS
AN EXTRA SPRIG TO
DECORATE
ICE CUBES
2 MEASURES GOLDEN RUM
2 MEASURES LIME JUICE
STRAWBERRY SLICE, TO
DECORATE

Muddle the strawberries, strawberry syrup and mint leaves in a cocktail shaker. Add some ice cubes, rum and lime juice and shake well. Double strain into a chilled slim Martini glass. Decorate with a strawberry slice and a mint sprig.

FIRST THE MONEY

1 LIME
1 TEASPOON WHITE CRÈME DE MENTHE
CRUSHED ICE
1 MEASURE DARK RUM
¾ MEASURE TOUSSAINT COFFEE LIQUEUR
COLA, TO TOP UP

Cut the lime into wedges and muddle with the crème de menthe in a highball glass. Fill the glass with crushed ice and add the rum and Toussaint. Top up with cola.

The really important things are said over cocktails and are never done.
PETER F DRUCKER

CUBAN BREEZE

Fill a highball glass with ice cubes and add the cranberry juice. Put some ice cubes into a cocktail shaker, add the rum and grapefruit juice and shake to mix. Strain the mixture over the cranberry juice and decorate with lime wedges.

ICE CUBES
3 MEASURES CRANBERRY JUICE
2 MEASURES HAVANA CLUB 3-YEAR-OLD RUM
2 MEASURES GRAPEFRUIT JUICE
LIME WEDGES, TO DECORATE

BERLIN BLONDE

Put some ice cubes into a cocktail shaker with the rum, Cointreau and cream. Shake well. Double strain into a chilled Martini glass. Decorate with a sprinkle of ground cinnamon and 2 cocktail cherries impaled on a cocktail stick.

ICE CUBES
1 MEASURE DARK RUM
1 MEASURE COINTREAU
1 MEASURE DOUBLE CREAM
GROUND CINNAMON, TO DECORATE
2 COCKTAIL CHERRIES, TO DECORATE

CHETTA'S PUNCH

ICE CUBES
2 MEASURES LAMB'S NAVY RUM
2 MEASURES BLACKCURRANT CORDIAL
1 TABLESPOON LEMON JUICE
6 DASHES ORANGE BITTERS
ORANGE SLICES, TO DECORATE

Put some ice cubes into a mixing glass with the rum, blackcurrant cordial, lemon juice and bitters and stir well. Strain into an old-fashioned glass filled with ice cubes and decorate with orange slices.

MAFIA MARTINI

ICE CUBES
2 MEASURES GOLDEN RUM
½ MEASURE CHAMBORD 1 MEASURE APPLE JUICE
LIME RIND TWIST, TO DECORATE

Put some ice cubes into a cocktail shaker with the rum, Chambord and apple juice and shake briefly. Double strain into a chilled Martini glass. Decorate with a lime rind twist.

Right: Mafia Martini

PIÑA COLADA

CRACKED ICE
1 MEASURE WHITE RUM
2 MEASURES COCONUT
MILK
2 MEASURES PINEAPPLE
JUICE
PINEAPPLE WEDGE, TO
DECORATE

Put some cracked ice into a cocktail shaker, with the rum, coconut milk and pineapple juice. Shake lightly to mix. Strain into a large glass and decorate with the pineapple wedge. Serve with long straws.

MONOLOCO ZOMBIE

ICE CUBES
1 MEASURE WHITE RUM
1 MEASURE NAVY RUM
½ MEASURE APRICOT
BRANDY
½ MEASURE ORANGE
CURAÇAO
2 MEASURES ORANGE
JUICE
2 MEASURES PINEAPPLE
JUICE
½ MEASURE LIME JUICE
1 DASH GRENADINE
½ MEASURE OVER-PROOF
RUM
PINEAPPLE WEDGES, TO
DECORATE

Put some ice cubes into a cocktail shaker with all the other ingredients, except the over-proof rum. Shake well. Strain over some ice cubes into a large hurricane glass. Top with the over-proof rum and decorate with pineapple wedges.

PINK TREASURE

Put the cracked ice, rum and cherry brandy into a glass. Add a splash of bitter lemon or soda water, if using. Decorate with a lemon rind spiral.

2 ICE CUBES, CRACKED
1 MEASURE WHITE RUM
1 MEASURE CHERRY BRANDY
BITTER LEMON OR SODA WATER, TO TASTE (OPTIONAL)
LEMON RIND SPIRAL, TO DECORATE

THE PAPA DOBLE

Put a scoop of crushed ice into a food processor or blender with the rum, Maraschino liqueur and fruit juices and blend until smooth. Serve in a highball glass with grapefruit wedges. This drink can be sweetened to taste with sugar syrup, although Hemingway never would.

CRUSHED ICE
3 MEASURES WHITE RUM
½ MEASURE MARASCHINO LIQUEUR
1 MEASURE LIME JUICE
1½ MEASURES GRAPEFRUIT JUICE
GRAPEFRUIT WEDGES, TO DECORATE

Left: The Papa Doble

ZOMBIE

ICE CUBES
1 MEASURE DARK RUM
1 MEASURE WHITE RUM
1/2 MEASURE GOLDEN RUM
1/2 MEASURE APRICOT BRANDY
JUICE OF 1/2 LIME
1 TEASPOON GRENADINE
2 MEASURES PINEAPPLE JUICE
1/2 MEASURE SUGAR SYRUP
2 TEASPOONS OVER-PROOF RUM
PINEAPPLE WEDGE AND LEAF, TO
DECORATE
SUGAR, TO DECORATE

Put some ice cubes into a cocktail shaker with the dark, white and golden rums, apricot brandy, lime juice, grenadine, pineapple juice and sugar syrup and shake well. Pour without straining into a chilled glass and float the over-proof rum on top. Decorate with a pineapple wedge and leaf, and sprinkle a pinch of sugar over the top.

GRENADA

4–5 ICE CUBES
JUICE OF 1/2 ORANGE
1 MEASURE SWEET
VERMOUTH
3 MEASURES GOLDEN OR
DARK RUM
CRUMBLED CINNAMON
STICK, TO DECORATE

Put the ice cubes into a mixing glass. Pour the orange juice, vermouth and rum over the ice. Stir vigorously, then strain into a chilled cocktail glass. Sprinkle a little crumbled cinnamon stick on top.

MY TIE COLLECTION

Put some ice cubes into a cocktail shaker with the golden rum, fruit juice, orgeat syrup and mint leaves and shake well. Strain over ice cubes into a highball glass, float the Navy rum on top and decorate with a cocktail cherry, a pineapple wedge and a lemon slice.

ICE CUBES
2 MEASURES GOLDEN RUM
1 MEASURE APPLE JUICE
½ MEASURE LIME JUICE
1 DASH ORGEAT SYRUP
6 MINT LEAVES
2 TEASPOONS WOOD'S NAVY RUM
COCKTAIL CHERRY, TO DECORATE
PINEAPPLE WEDGE, TO DECORATE
LEMON SLICE, TO DECORATE

LOBSTERS ON SOUTH BEACH

Put some crushed ice into a food processor or blender with the rums, mango purée, mandarin juice, coconut cream and pineapple chunks and blend until smooth. Serve in a large highball glass and decorate with a pineapple leaf and mango slices.

CRUSHED ICE
1 MEASURE WHITE RUM
1 MEASURE COCONUT RUM
1 MEASURE MANGO PURÉE
2 MEASURES MANDARIN JUICE (FRESH IF POSSIBLE)
1 MEASURE COCONUT CREAM
4 PINEAPPLE CHUNKS
PINEAPPLE LEAF, TO DECORATE
MANGO SLICES, TO DECORATE

BAHAMAS PUNCH

Pour the lemon juice and sugar syrup into a mixing glass. Shake in the bitters, then add the grenadine, rum and fruit. Stir and chill. To serve, fill an old-fashioned glass with cracked ice, pour in the punch without straining and sprinkle with grated nutmeg.

JUICE OF 1 LEMON
1 TEASPOON SUGAR SYRUP
3 DROPS ANGOSTURA BITTERS
½ TEASPOON GRENADINE
3 MEASURES GOLDEN OR WHITE RUM
ORANGE AND LEMON SLICES
CRACKED ICE
GRATED NUTMEG, TO DECORATE

EGG NOG

Half-fill a cocktail shaker with ice cubes. Add the egg, sugar syrup, rum and milk and shake well for about 1 minute. Strain into a tumbler and sprinkle with a little grated nutmeg and decorate with a cinnamon stick.

ICE CUBES
1 EGG
1 TABLESPOON SUGAR SYRUP
2 MEASURES RUM
6 MEASURES MILK
GRATED NUTMEG, TO DECORATE
CINNAMON STICK, TO DECORATE

Left: Egg Nog

BEAUTIFUL BETH

Put the ice cubes into a cocktail shaker. Pour the rum, Malibu and Cointreau over the ice and shake until a frost forms. Strain into an old-fashioned glass and top up with chilled cola. Decorate with a cherry.

3–4 ICE CUBES, CRUSHED
1 MEASURE LIGHT RUM
1 MEASURE MALIBU
½ MEASURE COINTREAU
CHILLED COLA, TO TOP UP
1 CHERRY, TO DECORATE

Left: Beautiful Beth

PASSION FOR FASHION

Put some ice cubes into a cocktail shaker. with the rum, Grand Marnier, bitters, passion fruit pulp and syrup and lime juice Shake well. Double strain into a chilled Martini glass. Decorate with passion fruit slice.

ICE CUBES
1½ MEASURES GOLDEN RUM
½ MEASURE GRAND MARNIER
2 DASHES ANGOSTURA BITTERS
PULP OF 1 PASSION FRUIT
2 TEASPOONS PASSION FRUIT SYRUP
1 DASH LIME JUICE
PASSION FRUIT SLICE, TO DECORATE

ST AUGUSTINE

ICE CUBES
1½ MEASURES WHITE RUM
1 MEASURE GRAPEFRUIT
JUICE
1 TEASPOON COINTREAU
CASTER SUGAR
LEMON RIND TWIST, TO
DECORATE

Put some ice cubes into a cocktail shaker and pour over the rum, grapefruit juice and Cointreau over them. Shake well. Frost the rim of a glass by dipping it into water, then pressing it into the sugar. Strain the drink into the prepared glass. Add ice cubes and a lemon rind twist.

TROPICAL DREAM

3–4 ICE CUBES
1 MEASURE WHITE RUM
1 MEASURE MIDORI
1 TABLESPOON COCONUT CREAM
3 TABLESPOONS PINEAPPLE JUICE
3 TABLESPOONS ORANGE JUICE
½ MEASURE CRÈME DE BANANE
½ BANANA
BANANA WEDGE WITH SKIN ON, TO
DECORATE

Put the ice cubes into a food processor or blender with the rum, Midori, coconut cream and fruit juices. Blend for about 10 seconds. Add the crème de banane and the banana and blend for a further 10 seconds. Pour into a tall glass, decorate with a banana wedge and serve with long straws.

Right: Tropical Dream
(right)

YELLOW BIRD

Put some ice cubes into a cocktail shaker. Pour in the rum, lime juice, Galliano and Triple Sec and shake well. Strain into a chilled cocktail glass.

ICE CUBES
1½ MEASURES RUM
1 MEASURE LIME JUICE
½ MEASURE GALLIANO
½ MEASURE TRIPLE SEC

PLANTER'S PUNCH

Put some ice cubes into a cocktail shaker with the rum, bitters, lime juice, chilled water and sugar syrup. Shake well. Strain into a highball glass filled with ice cubes. Decorate with orange and lime slices.

ICE CUBES
2 MEASURES MYER'S JAMAICAN PLANTER'S PUNCH RUM
4 DROPS ANGOSTURA BITTERS
½ MEASURE LIME JUICE
2 MEASURES CHILLED WATER
1 MEASURE SUGAR SYRUP
ORANGE AND LIME SLICES, TO DECORATE

Left: Planter's Punch

FOXY'S MILLENNIUM PUNCH

ICE CUBES
1½ MEASURES WHITE RUM
1 MEASURE DARK RUM
2 MEASURES CRANBERRY JUICE
2 MEASURES GUAVA JUICE
½ MEASURE LIME JUICE
PINEAPPLE AND LIME SLICES, TO DECORATE
COCKTAIL CHERRY, TO DECORATE

Put some ice cubes into a large highball glass. Pour the rums and fruit juices over the ice and stir. Decorate with pineapple and lime slices and a cocktail cherry, spiked on a cocktail stick.

AFTER DARK CRUSH

CRUSHED ICE
2 MEASURES BARBADIAN RUM
½ MEASURE KOKO KANU (COCONUT RUM)
½ MEASURE VANILLA SYRUP
1 MEASURE COCONUT CREAM
SODA WATER, TO TOP UP
COCKTAIL CHERRIES, TO DECORATE

Fill a sling glass with crushed ice, then add, one by one, in order, the rums, vanilla syrup and coconut cream. Stir and top up with soda water. Add more ice and decorate with cocktail cherries. Serve with long straws.

BOSSA NOVA

ICE CUBES
2 MEASURES WHITE RUM
½ MEASURE GALLIANO
½ MEASURE APRICOT
BRANDY
4 MEASURES PRESSED
APPLE JUICE
1 MEASURE LIME JUICE
½ MEASURE SUGAR SYRUP
LIME WEDGES, SPLIT, TO
DECORATE

Put some ice cubes into a cocktail shaker with the rum, Galliano, apricot brandy, fruit juices and sugar syrup and shake well. Strain into a highball glass filled with ice cubes. Decorate with split lime wedges and serve with long straws.

BRANDY

TOULON

4–5 ICE CUBES
1 MEASURE DRY
VERMOUTH
1 MEASURE BÉNÉDICTINE
3 MEASURES BRANDY
ORANGE RIND STRIP, TO
DECORATE

Put the ice cubes into a mixing glass. Pour the vermouth, Bénédictine and brandy over the ice and stir vigorously. Strain into a chilled cocktail glass and decorate with an orange rind strip.

AMERICAN ROSE

4–5 ICE CUBES, PLUS
CRUSHED ICE, TO SERVE
1 MEASURE BRANDY
1 DASH PERNOD
1 DASH GRENADINE
½ RIPE PEACH, SKINNED,
STONED AND ROUGHLY
CHOPPED
CHAMPAGNE, TO TOP UP
PEACH OR MANGO SLICES,
TO DECORATE

Put the ice cubes into a cocktail shaker. Pour in the brandy, Pernod and grenadine and add the peach. Shake well, then strain into a cocktail or Margarita glass filled with crushed ice. Top up with Champagne just before serving and add peach or mango slices to decorate.

SHANGHAI

3 ICE CUBES, CRUSHED
1 MEASURE BRANDY
½ MEASURE CURAÇAO
¼ MEASURE MARASCHINO
LIQUEUR
2 DASHES ANGOSTURA
BITTERS
LEMON RIND SPIRAL, TO
DECORATE
COCKTAIL CHERRY, TO
DECORATE

Put the crushed ice into a cocktail shaker. Add the brandy, Curaçao, Maraschino liqueur and bitters and shake to mix. Pour into a cocktail glass and decorate with a lemon rind spiral and a cocktail cherry impaled on a cocktail stick.

MELBOURNE

4–5 ICE CUBES
1 MEASURE CURAÇAO
3 MEASURES BRANDY
LEMON RIND, TO
DECORATE

Put the ice cubes into a mixing glass, pour over the Curaçao and brandy and stir vigorously. Strain into a chilled cocktail glass. Squeeze the zest from the lemon rind over the surface, then drop it in.

FIFTH AVENUE

1 MEASURE BROWN CRÈME
DE CACAO
1 MEASURE APRICOT
BRANDY
1 MEASURE SINGLE CREAM

Pour the crème de cacao into a straight-sided liqueur glass. Using the back of a bar spoon, slowly float the apricot brandy over the crème de cacao. Pour the cream over the apricot brandy in the same way.

CORPSE REVIVER

3 ICE CUBES, CRACKED
2 MEASURES BRANDY
1 MEASURE CALVADOS
1 MEASURE SWEET
VERMOUTH
APPLE SLICE, TO
DECORATE

Put the cracked ice into a cocktail shaker. Add the brandy, Calvados and vermouth and shake until a frost forms. Strain into a glass and decorate with an apple slice.

BANANA BLISS

4–5 ICE CUBES
1 MEASURE BRANDY
1 MEASURE CRÈME DE
BANANE
1 MEASURE COINTREAU
1 MEASURE LEMON JUICE
BANANA WEDGE, TO
DECORATE

Put the ice cubes into a mixing glass and pour over the brandy, crème de banane and Cointreau. Stir with a spoon, then strain into a cocktail glass. Dip the banana wedge in lemon juice to prevent it discolouring and attach it to the rim of the glass.

PENGUIN

1 MEASURE BRANDY
½ MEASURE COINTREAU
1 MEASURE LEMON JUICE
1 MEASURE ORANGE JUICE
1 DASH GRENADINE
ICE CUBES
¼ SLICE OF ORANGE, TO DECORATE
¼ SLICE OF LEMON, TO DECORATE

Pour the brandy, Cointreau, fruit juices and grenadine into a mixing glass and stir well. Pour into a tall glass filled with ice cubes. Decorate with the orange and lemon slice quarters placed on the rim of the glass. Serve with 2 long straws.

HAITI PUNCH

2 PINEAPPLES, PEELED AND CUBED
3 LEMONS, SLICED
3 ORANGES, SLICED
300 ML (½ PINT) BRANDY
300 ML (½ PINT) ORANGE NASSAU LIQUEUR
2 BOTTLES SPARKLING DRY WHITE WINE
PINEAPPLE LEAVES, TO DECORATE
ORANGE RIND SPIRALS, TO DECORATE

Put the prepared fruit into a large bowl or jug and pour the brandy and Orange Nassau over it. Cover and chill for several hours. To serve, pour about 1 measure of the brandy mixture into a Champagne flute or tall glass, top up with sparkling wine and add some of the pineapple cubes. Decorate with a pineapple leaf and an orange rind spiral. Serves 12–15.

One revolution is like one cocktail, it just gets you organized for the next.
WILL ROGERS

Right: Haiti Punch

BRANDIED BOAT

CRUSHED ICE
1 MEASURE BRANDY
2 TEASPOONS LEMON
JUICE
1 TEASPOON MARASCHINO
BITTERS
1 MEASURE PORT
LEMON RIND SPIRAL, TO
DECORATE

Put some crushed ice into a cocktail shaker. Add the brandy, lemon juice and bitters and shake to mix. Pour into a tumbler and then pour the port over the drink. Decorate with a lemon rind spiral on the side.

SPICED SIDECAR

ICE CUBES
JUICE OF ½ LEMON
2 MEASURES CAPTAIN
MORGAN ORIGINAL
SPICED RUM
1 MEASURE BRANDY
1 MEASURE COINTREAU
LEMON AND ORANGE RIND
TWISTS, TO DECORATE

Put some ice cubes into a cocktail shaker with the lemon juice, rum, brandy and Cointreau and shake well. Strain into an old-fashioned glass filled with ice cubes and decorate with lemon and orange rind twists.

BIG CITY DOG

2 DASHES PEYCHAUD'S
BITTERS
ICE CUBES
1 MEASURE BRANDY
½ MEASURE GREEN
CHARTREUSE
½ MEASURE CHERRY
BRANDY

Put the bitters into a brandy balloon and swirl them around to coat the inside. Turn the glass upside down and let it drain. Put some ice cubes into a mixing glass with the brandy, Chartreuse and cherry brandy and stir well. Double strain into the brandy balloon.

ANGEL FACE

3 ICE CUBES, CRACKED
1 MEASURE GIN
1 MEASURE APRICOT
BRANDY
1 MEASURE CALVADOS
ORANGE RIND TWIST, TO
DECORATE

Put the cracked ice into a cocktail shaker and pour the gin, apricot brandy and Calvados over it. Shake well. Strain into a cocktail glass and decorate with an orange rind twist.

METROPOLITAN

The trouble with jogging is that the ice falls out of your glass.
MARTIN MULL

CRACKED ICE
1 MEASURE BRANDY
1 MEASURE SWEET VERMOUTH
½ TEASPOON SUGAR SYRUP
3–4 DASHES ANGOSTURA BITTERS

Put some cracked ice into a cocktail shaker with the brandy, vermouth, sugar syrup and bitters and shake well. Strain into a chilled cocktail glass.

Left: Metropolitan

CHRISTMAS PUNCH

JUICE OF 15 LEMONS
JUICE OF 4 ORANGES
625 G (1 LB 6 OZ) SUGAR
ICE CUBES
300 ML (½ PINT) ORANGE CURAÇAO
2 MEASURES GRENADINE
2 MEASURES BRANDY
2.5 LITRES (4½ PINTS) SPARKLING MINERAL WATER
ORANGE OR LEMON RIND SPIRAL, TO DECORATE

Pour the fruit juices into a jug. Add the sugar and stir gently until it has dissolved. Put a large quantity of ice cubes into a large punch bowl. Add the fruit juices, Curaçao, grenadine, brandy and mineral water and stir well. Decorate with orange or lemon rind spiral before serving. Serves 15–20.

BRANDY CRUSTA

LEMON WEDGE
CASTER SUGAR
ICE CUBES
2 MEASURES BRANDY
½ MEASURE ORANGE
CURAÇAO
½ MEASURE MARASCHINO
LIQUEUR
1 MEASURE LEMON JUICE
3 DASHES ANGOSTURA
BITTERS
LEMON RIND SPIRAL, TO
DECORATE

Frost the rim of a chilled cocktail glass by moistening it with the lemon wedge and pressing it in the sugar. Put some ice cubes into a cocktail shaker with the brandy, Curaçao, Maraschino liqueur, lemon juice and bitters and shake well. Strain into the prepared glass.

BETWEEN THE SHEETS

4–5 ICE CUBES
1¼ MEASURES BRANDY
1 MEASURE WHITE RUM
½ MEASURE COINTREAU
¾ MEASURE LEMON JUICE
½ MEASURE SUGAR SYRUP

Put the ice cubes into a cocktail shaker. Add the brandy, rum, Cointreau, lemon juice and sugar syrup and shake until a frost forms. Strain the drink into a chilled cocktail glass.

APPLE POSSET

8 MEASURES
UNSWEETENED APPLE
JUICE
1 TEASPOON SOFT BROWN
SUGAR
2 TABLESPOONS
CALVADOS
CINNAMON STICK

Heat the apple juice in a small saucepan to just below boiling point. Meanwhile, measure the sugar and Calvados into a warmed mug or glass. Pour the hot apple juice over the sugar and Calvados, stirring with the cinnamon stick until the sugar has dissolved.

BURNT ORANGE

4–5 ICE CUBES
3 DROPS ORANGE BITTERS
OR ANGOSTURA BITTERS
JUICE OF ½ ORANGE
3 MEASURES BRANDY
¼ SLICE OF ORANGE, TO
DECORATE

Put the ice cubes into a cocktail shaker. Shake the bitters over the ice, add the orange juice and brandy and shake vigorously. Strain into a chilled cocktail glass and decorate with a quarter slice of orange.

MONTA ROSA

4–5 ICE CUBES
JUICE OF ½ LIME
1 MEASURE COINTREAU
3 MEASURES BRANDY

Put the ice cubes into a mixing glass. Pour the lime juice, Cointreau and brandy over the ice and stir vigorously. Strain into a chilled cocktail glass.

ANGEL'S KISS

½ MEASURE CRÈME DE CACAO
½ MEASURE BRANDY
½ MEASURE LIGHTLY WHIPPED DOUBLE CREAM

Pour the crème de cacao into a shot glass. Using the back of a bar spoon, slowly float the brandy over the crème de cacao. Pour the cream over the brandy in the same way.

CAEN-CAEN

4–5 ICE CUBES
2 MEASURES BRANDY
1 MEASURE CALVADOS
½ MEASURE SWEET
VERMOUTH

Put the ice cubes into a mixing glass. Pour the brandy, Calvados and vermouth over the ice and stir vigorously. Strain into a chilled cocktail glass.

BRANDY SIDECAR

4–5 ICE CUBES
JUICE OF 1 LEMON
1 MEASURE COINTREAU
2 MEASURES BRANDY
ORANGE SLICE, TO
DECORATE

Put the ice cubes into a mixing glass. Pour the lemon juice, Cointreau and brandy over the ice and stir vigorously. Strain into a chilled cocktail glass. Decorate with an orange slice.

HOP FROG

ICE CUBES
1 MEASURE BRANDY
2 MEASURES LIME JUICE

Put some ice cubes into a cocktail shaker with all the other ingredients and shake well. Strain into a chilled cocktail glass.

EAST INDIA

ICE CUBES
3 DROPS ANGOSTURA BITTERS
½ MEASURE PINEAPPLE JUICE
½ MEASURE BLUE CURAÇAO
2 MEASURES BRANDY
ORANGE RIND SPIRAL, TO DECORATE

Put some ice cubes into a mixing glass. Shake the bitters over the ice and pour the pineapple juice, Curaçao and brandy over it. Stir until frothy, then strain into a chilled cocktail glass. Decorate with an orange rind spiral tied into a knot.

AVONDALE HABIT

3 STRAWBERRIES, HULLED
1 DASH SUGAR SYRUP
4 MINT LEAVES
CRUSHED ICE
1½ MEASURES BRANDY
FRESHLY CRACKED BLACK PEPPER
2 TEASPOONS CRÈME DE MENTHE
MINT SPRIG, TO DECORATE
STRAWBERRY HALF, TO DECORATE

Muddle the strawberries, sugar syrup and mint leaves in an old-fashioned glass. Almost fill the glass with crushed ice, then add the brandy and black pepper. Stir and add more crushed ice, then add the crème de menthe. Decorate with a mint sprig and a strawberry half.

STINGER

4 ICE CUBES, CRACKED
½ MEASURE WHITE CRÈME DE MENTHE
1½ MEASURES BRANDY
MINT SPRIG, TO DECORATE

Put the cracked ice into a cocktail shaker and pour the crème de menthe and brandy over it. Shake well. Strain into a cocktail or Margarita glass and decorate with a mint sprig.

LEO

2–3 ICE CUBES, CRUSHED
1 MEASURE BRANDY
1½ MEASURES ORANGE JUICE
½ MEASURE AMARETTO DI SARONNO LIQUEUR
SODA WATER, TO TASTE
1 TEASPOON CAMPARI

Put the crushed ice into a cocktail shaker. Add the brandy, orange juice and Amaretto di Saronno and shake well. Strain into a tall glass and add soda water, to taste, and the Campari.

TIDAL WAVE

6 ICE CUBES
1 MEASURE MANDARINE NAPOLÉON BRANDY
4 MEASURES BITTER LEMON
1 DASH LEMON JUICE
LEMON SLICE, TO DECORATE

Put the ice cubes into a highball glass. Add the Mandarine Napoléon, bitter lemon and lemon juice and stir gently. Decorate with a lemon slice.

APRICOT SOUR

2 ICE CUBES, CRACKED
1 MEASURE APRICOT BRANDY
1 MEASURE LEMON JUICE
1 DASH ANGOSTURA BITTERS
1 DASH EGG WHITE
1 APRICOT WEDGE, CHOPPED
LEMON SLICE, TO DECORATE
COCKTAIL CHERRY, TO DECORATE

Put all the ingredients into a cocktail shaker and shake vigorously. Strain into a tumbler and decorate with a lemon slice and a cocktail cherry impaled on a cocktail stick.

BRANDY FIX

1 TEASPOON ICING SUGAR
1 TEASPOON WATER
1 MEASURE BRANDY
½ MEASURE CHERRY BRANDY
JUICE OF ½ LEMON
CRUSHED ICE
LEMON SLICE, TO DECORATE

Dissolve the sugar in the water in a mixing glass, then add the brandy, cherry brandy and lemon juice. Stir to mix. Pour into a brandy balloon or small tumbler. Fill the glass with crushed ice, float a lemon slice on top.

HARLEQUIN

LIGHTLY BEATEN EGG WHITE
CASTER SUGAR
1 MEASURE KIRSCH
1 MEASURE APRICOT BRANDY
2 MEASURES ORANGE JUICE
SODA WATER, TO TOP UP
ORANGE SLICE, TO DECORATE
2 COCKTAIL CHERRIES, TO DECORATE

Frost the rim of a tumbler by dipping it into the egg white, then pressing it into the sugar. Pour the kirsch, apricot brandy and orange juice into a cocktail shaker. Shake lightly. Strain into the prepared glass and top up with soda water. Decorate with an orange slice and cocktail cherries.

PARISIEN

CRUSHED ICE
1 MEASURE BRANDY
½ MEASURE CALVADOS
1 MEASURE LEMON JUICE
SUGAR SYRUP, TO TASTE
½ MEASURE POIRE WILLIAM LIQUEUR
APPLE AND PEAR SLICES, OR SEASONAL FRUITS,
TO DECORATE
MINT SPRIG, TO DECORATE

Fill a tumbler with crushed ice. Add the brandy, Calvados, lemon juice and sugar syrup to taste. Pour the Poire William over the top and decorate with the fruit and mint sprig. Serve with a straw.

Left: Parisien

BRANDY CUBAN

2–3 ICE CUBES
1½ MEASURES BRANDY
JUICE OF ½ LIME
COLA, TO TOP UP
LIME SLICE, TO DECORATE

Put the ice cubes into a tumbler and pour the brandy and lime juice over them. Stir vigorously to mix. Top up with cola and decorate with a lime slice. Serve with a straw.

MONTE CARLO SLING

5 SEEDLESS GRAPES, PLUS EXTRA
TO DECORATE
CRUSHED ICE
1 MEASURE BRANDY
½ MEASURE PEACH LIQUEUR
1 MEASURE RUBY PORT
1 MEASURE LEMON JUICE
½ MEASURE ORANGE JUICE
1 DASH ORANGE BITTERS
2 MEASURES CHAMPAGNE

Muddle the grapes in a tall glass, then fill the glass with crushed ice. Put all the other ingredients, except the Champagne, into a cocktail shaker and add more ice. Shake well and strain into the glass. Top up with Champagne and decorate with grapes.

BEDTIME BOUNCER

2 MEASURES BRANDY
1 MEASURE COINTREAU
5 MEASURES BITTER
LEMON
4–6 ICE CUBES
LEMON RIND TWIST, TO
DECORATE

Pour the brandy, Cointreau and bitter lemon into a tumbler, stir well and add the ice cubes. Decorate with a lemon rind twist and serve with a straw.

BRANDY FLIP

ICE CUBES
1 EGG
2 MEASURES BRANDY
1½ TEASPOONS CASTER
SUGAR
GRATED NUTMEG, TO
DECORATE

Put some ice cubes into a cocktail shaker with the egg, brandy and sugar and shake well. Strain the drink into a brandy balloon and sprinkle a little grated nutmeg on top.

BRANDY CLASSIC

4–5 ICE CUBES, PLUS CRACKED ICE TO SERVE
1 MEASURE BRANDY
1 MEASURE BLUE CURAÇAO
1 MEASURE MARASCHINO LIQUEUR
JUICE OF ½ LEMON
LEMON WEDGE, TO DECORATE

Put the ice cubes into a cocktail shaker. Pour in the brandy, Curaçao, Maraschino liqueur and lemon juice and shake to mix. Strain into a chilled cocktail glass. Add some cracked ice and a lemon wedge.

FROM THE RAFTERS

ICE CUBES
1 MEASURE BRANDY
1 TABLESPOON FRANGELICO HAZELNUT LIQUEUR
1 MEASURE COINTREAU
1 MEASURE PINEAPPLE JUICE
CHERRY SLICES, TO DECORATE

Put some ice cubes into a cocktail shaker with the brandy, Frangelico, Cointreau and pineapple juice and shake to mix. Strain into a chilled cocktail glass and decorate with cherry slices, which will sink to the bottom of the glass.

AMERICAN BEAUTY

4–5 ICE CUBES
1 MEASURE BRANDY
1 MEASURE DRY VERMOUTH
1 MEASURE ORANGE JUICE
1 MEASURE GRENADINE
1 DASH CRÈME DE MENTHE
2–3 DASHES RUBY PORT
COCKTAIL CHERRY, TO
DECORATE
ORANGE SLICE, TO
DECORATE
MINT SPRIG, TO DECORATE

Put the ice cubes into a cocktail shaker. Pour in the brandy, vermouth, orange juice, grenadine and crème de menthe and shake well. Strain into a cocktail glass. Tilt the glass and gently pour in a little ruby port so that it floats on top. Decorate with a cocktail cherry, an orange slice and a mint sprig impaled on a cocktail stick.

MORNING

4–5 ICE CUBES
3 DASHES ANGOSTURA
BITTERS
5 DASHES PERNOD
½ TEASPOON GRENADINE
½ TEASPOON DRY
VERMOUTH
1 MEASURE CURAÇAO
3 MEASURES BRANDY
COCKTAIL CHERRIES, TO
DECORATE

Put the ice cubes into a cocktail shaker. Shake the bitters over the ice and add the Pernod. Pour in the grenadine, vermouth, Curaçao and brandy, shake well, then strain into a chilled cocktail or Margarita glass. Decorate with cherries impaled on a cocktail stick.

APPLEJACK SOUR

ICE CUBES
2 MEASURES APPLE
BRANDY
½ MEASURE LEMON JUICE
1½ TEASPOONS SUGAR
SYRUP

Put some ice cubes into a cocktail shaker and pour the apple brandy, lemon juice and sugar syrup over them. Shake well. Strain into a sour glass and serve straight up or in an old-fashioned glass over ice.

SANGRIA

ICE CUBES
2 BOTTLES LIGHT SPANISH RED
WINE, CHILLED
4 MEASURES BRANDY
450 ML (16 FL OZ) SODA WATER,
CHILLED
FRUIT IN SEASON, SUCH AS APPLES,
PEARS, LEMONS, PEACHES AND
STRAWBERRIES, SLICED
ORANGE OR LIME SLICES, TO
DECORATE

Put some ice cubes into a large bowl and pour the wine and brandy over them. Stir. Add the soda water and float the fruit on top. Serve in tall glasses and decorate with orange or lime slices. Serves 10–12.

Right: Sangria

JAFFA

3 ICE CUBES, CRACKED
1 MEASURE MANDARINE NAPOLÉON BRANDY
1 MEASURE BROWN CRÈME DE CACAO
1 MEASURE SINGLE CREAM
COCOA POWDER, TO DECORATE

Put the cracked ice into a cocktail shaker with the brandy, crème de cacao and cream and shake well. Strain into a chilled cocktail glass and sprinkle with cocoa powder.

BRANDY ALEXANDER

3 ICE CUBES, CRACKED
1 MEASURE BRANDY
1 MEASURE BROWN CRÈME DE CACAO
1 MEASURE SINGLE CREAM
COCOA POWDER, TO DECORATE
COFFEE BEANS, TO DECORATE

Put the cracked ice into a cocktail shaker with the brandy, crème de cacao and cream and shake well. Strain into a chilled cocktail glass, float a couple of coffee beans on the surface and sprinkle with cocoa powder.

Left: Brandy Alexander

FISH HOUSE PUNCH

ICE CUBES
1 MEASURE BRANDY
1 MEASURE PEACH BRANDY
1 MEASURE GOLDEN RUM
1 MEASURE LEMON JUICE
1 MEASURE COLD ENGLISH
BREAKFAST TEA
½ MEASURE SUGAR SYRUP
SODA WATER, TO TOP UP
LEMON SLICE, TO
DECORATE

Put some ice cubes into a cocktail shaker with the brandies, rum, lemon juice, tea and sugar syrup. Shake well. Double strain into a highball glass filled with ice cubes. Top up with soda water, decorate with a lemon slice and serve with straws.

THE PUDDING COCKTAIL

1 MEASURE CALVADOS
1½ MEASURES BRANDY
1 EGG YOLK
1 TEASPOON CASTER SUGAR
ICE CUBES
GROUND CINNAMON, TO DECORATE

Put the Calvados, brandy, egg yolk and sugar into a cocktail shaker with some ice cubes and shake until well mixed. Strain into a chilled cocktail glass. Light a long taper, hold it over the glass and sprinkle cinnamon through the flame on to the surface of the drink.

NICE PEAR

ICE CUBES
2 MEASURES BRANDY
1 MEASURE POIRE WILLIAM LIQUEUR
1 MEASURE SWEET VERMOUTH
PEELED PEAR SLICES, TO DECORATE

Put some ice cubes into a cocktail shaker with the brandy, Poire William and vermouth and shake well. Strain into a chilled cocktail glass and decorate with pear slices.

> The cocktail party is a device for paying off obligations to people you don't want to invite for dinner.
> **CHARLES SMITH**

GIN

SWEET SIXTEEN

6–8 ICE CUBES
2 MEASURES GIN
JUICE OF ½ LIME
2 DASHES GRENADINE
1 TEASPOON SUGAR SYRUP
BITTER LEMON, TO TOP UP
LEMON RIND STRIP, TO
DECORATE

Put half the ice cubes into a cocktail shaker and pour the gin, lime juice, grenadine and sugar syrup over them. Shake until a frost forms. Put the remaining ice cubes into a highball glass, strain the cocktail over the ice and top up with bitter lemon. Decorate with a lemon rind strip.

GIMLET

2 MEASURES GIN
1 MEASURE LIME CORDIAL
ICE CUBES
½ MEASURE WATER
JUICE OF ¼ LIME
LIME RIND SPIRAL, TO
DECORATE

Put the gin and lime cordial into a mixing glass, fill up with ice cubes and stir well. Strain into a chilled cocktail glass and add the water and lime juice into the cocktail. Decorate with a lime rind spiral.

Right: Gimlet

MOON RIVER

4–5 ICE CUBES
½ MEASURE DRY GIN
½ MEASURE APRICOT BRANDY
½ MEASURE COINTREAU
¼ MEASURE GALLIANO
¼ MEASURE LEMON JUICE
COCKTAIL CHERRY, TO DECORATE

Put the ice cubes into a mixing glass. Pour the gin, apricot brandy, Cointreau, Galliano and lemon juice over the ice, stir, then strain into a large, chilled cocktail glass. Decorate with a cocktail cherry.

LUIGI

ICE CUBES
1 MEASURE ORANGE JUICE
1 MEASURE DRY VERMOUTH
½ MEASURE COINTREAU
1 MEASURE GRENADINE
2 MEASURES GIN
BLOOD ORANGE SLICE, TO DECORATE

Put some ice cubes into a mixing glass. Pour the orange juice, vermouth, Cointreau, grenadine and gin over the ice and stir vigorously. Strain into a chilled cocktail glass. Decorate with a blood orange slice.

BITTERSWEET SYMPHONY

ICE CUBES
1 MEASURE GIN
1 MEASURE CAMPARI
½ MEASURE PASSION FRUIT
SYRUP
½ MEASURE LEMON JUICE
LEMON SLICES, TO DECORATE

Put some ice cubes into a cocktail shaker with the gin, Campari, passion fruit syrup and lemon juice and shake to mix. Strain into an old-fashioned glass over 4–6 ice cubes and decorate with lemon slices.

NEGRONI

ICE CUBES
1 MEASURE PLYMOUTH GIN
1 MEASURE CAMPARI
1 MEASURE RED VERMOUTH
SODA WATER, TO TOP UP
(OPTIONAL)
ORANGE SLICES, TO
DECORATE

Put some ice cubes into a cocktail shaker with the gin, Campari and vermouth and shake to mix. Strain into an old-fashioned glass filled with ice cubes, top up with soda water, if you like, and decorate with orange slices.

BY INVITATION ONLY

3 MEASURES GIN
2 TEASPOONS SUGAR SYRUP
2 TEASPOONS LIME JUICE
1 EGG WHITE
ICE CUBES
1 TABLESPOON CRÈME DE MURE
BLACKBERRIES, TO DECORATE

Put the gin, sugar syrup, lime juice and egg white into a cocktail shaker and shake to mix. Strain into a highball glass filled with ice cubes and lace with the crème de mure. Decorate with blackberries.

HONOLULU

4–5 ICE CUBES
1 MEASURE PINEAPPLE JUICE
1 MEASURE LEMON JUICE
1 MEASURE ORANGE JUICE
½ TEASPOON GRENADINE
3 MEASURES GIN
PINEAPPLE SLICE, TO DECORATE
COCKTAIL CHERRY, TO DECORATE

Put the ice cubes into a cocktail shaker and pour the fruit juices, grenadine and gin over them. Shake until a frost forms. Strain into a chilled cocktail glass and decorate with a pineapple slice and a cocktail cherry.

RED CLOUD

ICE CUBES
1½ MEASURES GIN
2 TEASPOONS APRICOT LIQUEUR
2 TEASPOONS LEMON JUICE
1 TEASPOON GRENADINE
1–2 DASHES ANGOSTURA
BITTERS

Put some ice cubes into a cocktail shaker and pour the gin, apricot liqueur, lemon juice, grenadine and bitters over them. Shake well, strain into a glass and add more ice cubes.

NEW ORLEANS DRY MARTINI

5–6 ICE CUBES
2–3 DROPS PERNOD
1 MEASURE DRY VERMOUTH
4 MEASURES GIN

Put the ice cubes into a mixing glass. Pour the Pernod over the ice, then pour in the vermouth and gin. Stir (never shake) vigorously and evenly without splashing. Strain into a chilled cocktail glass.

DELFT DONKEY

3–4 ICE CUBES, CRACKED
2 MEASURES GIN
JUICE OF 1 LEMON
GINGER BEER, TO TOP UP
LEMON SLICE, TO DECORATE

Put the cracked ice into a cocktail shaker and pour the gin and lemon juice over it. Shake until a frost forms. Pour into a hurricane glass or large tumbler and top up with ginger beer. Decorate with a lemon slice and serve with a straw.

SAPPHIRE MARTINI

4 ICE CUBES
2 MEASURES GIN
½ MEASURE BLUE CURAÇAO
RED OR BLUE COCKTAIL CHERRY,
TO DECORATE
MINT LEAF, TO DECORATE

Put the ice cubes into a cocktail shaker. Pour in the gin and Curaçao. Shake well to mix. Strain into a cocktail glass and decorate with a cocktail cherry and mint leaf impaled on a cocktail stick.

Right: Sapphire Martini

ZAZA

5–6 ICE CUBES
3 DROPS ORANGE BITTERS
1 MEASURE DUBONNET
2 MEASURES GIN

Put the ice cubes into a mixing glass. Shake the bitters over the ice, pour in the Dubonnet and gin and stir vigorously without splashing. Strain into a chilled cocktail glass.

PINK CLOVER CLUB

4–5 ICE CUBES
JUICE OF 1 LIME
1 DASH GRENADINE
1 EGG WHITE
3 MEASURES GIN
STRAWBERRY SLICE, TO
DECORATE

Put the ice cubes into a cocktail shaker. Pour the lime juice, grenadine, egg white and gin over the ice. Shake until a frost forms, then strain into a cocktail glass. Decorate with a strawberry slice and serve with a straw.

TURF

ICE CUBES
1 MEASURE GIN
1 MEASURE DRY VERMOUTH
1 TEASPOON LEMON JUICE
1 TEASPOON PERNOD
LEMON SLICE, TO DECORATE

Put some ice cubes into a cocktail shaker and pour the gin, vermouth, lemon juice and Pernod over them. Shake well, then strain into a glass containing more ice cubes. Decorate with a lemon slice.

GIN CUP

3 MINT SPRIGS, PLUS EXTRA
TO DECORATE
1 TEASPOON SUGAR SYRUP
CRACKED ICE
JUICE OF ½ LEMON
3 MEASURES GIN

Muddle the mint and sugar syrup in an old-fashioned glass. Fill the glass with cracked ice, add the lemon juice and gin and stir until a frost begins to form. Decorate with extra mint sprigs.

RUBY FIZZ

ICE CUBES
JUICE OF ½ LEMON
1 TEASPOON GRANULATED SUGAR
1 EGG WHITE
2 MEASURES SLOE GIN
2 DASHES RASPBERRY SYRUP OR
GRENADINE
SODA WATER, TO TOP UP

Put some ice cubes into a cocktail shaker. Add the lemon juice, sugar, egg white, gin and raspberry syrup or grenadine. Shake well, strain into a tall tumbler and top up with the soda water.

MBOLERO

2 LIME WEDGES
2 MEASURES GIN
6 MINT LEAVES, PLUS AN EXTRA
SPRIG TO DECORATE
6 DROPS ORANGE BITTERS
1 DASH SUGAR SYRUP
ICE CUBES

Squeeze the lime wedges into a cocktail shaker. Add the gin, mint leaves, bitters, sugar syrup and some ice cubes and shake well. Double strain into a chilled Martini glass. Decorate with a mint sprig.

Right: Mbolero

PARADISE

3 ICE CUBES, CRACKED
1 DASH LEMON JUICE
½ MEASURE ORANGE JUICE
1 MEASURE GIN
½ MEASURE APRICOT BRANDY
ORANGE AND LEMON SLICES, TO
DECORATE

Put the cracked ice into a cocktail shaker. Pour over the fruit juices, gin and apricot brandy and shake well. Strain into a chilled cocktail glass and decorate with orange and lemon slices.

MONKEY GLAND

3–4 ICE CUBES
1 MEASURE ORANGE JUICE
2 MEASURES GIN
3 DASHES PERNOD
3 DASHES GRENADINE

Put the ice cubes into a cocktail shaker with the orange juice, gin, Pernod and grenadine. Shake well, then strain the drink into a chilled cocktail glass.

Left: Monkey Gland

STORMY WEATHER

3 ICE CUBES, CRACKED
1½ MEASURES GIN
¼ MEASURE MANDARINE NAPOLÉON
BRANDY
¼ MEASURE DRY VERMOUTH
¼ MEASURE SWEET VERMOUTH
ORANGE RIND SPIRAL, TO DECORATE

Put the cracked ice into a cocktail shaker and add the gin, Mandarine Napoléon and vermouths. Shake to mix and strain into a chilled cocktail glass. Decorate the rim of the glass with an orange rind spiral.

BIJOU

3 ICE CUBES
1 MEASURE GIN
½ MEASURE GREEN CHARTREUSE
½ MEASURE SWEET VERMOUTH
1 DASH ORANGE BITTERS
LEMON RIND SPIRAL, TO DECORATE

Put the ice cubes into a mixing glass and add the gin, Chartreuse, vermouth and bitters. Stir well and strain into a cocktail glass. Squeeze the zest from the lemon rind over the surface and drop it in.

Right: Bijou

PARK LANE SPECIAL

ICE CUBES
2 MEASURES GIN
½ MEASURE APRICOT BRANDY
½ MEASURE ORANGE JUICE
1 DASH GRENADINE
½ EGG WHITE

Put some ice cubes into a cocktail shaker and pour all the other ingredients over them. Shake well and strain into a cocktail glass.

SMOKY

ICE CUBES
¼ MEASURE DRY VERMOUTH
2 MEASURES GIN
1 MEASURE SLOE GIN
5 DROPS ORANGE BITTERS
ORANGE RIND TWIST, TO DECORATE

Put ice cubes into a mixing glass, add the vermouth and stir until the ice cubes are well coated. Pour in the gin, sloe gin and bitters and stir well, then strain into a chilled cocktail glass and add an orange rind twist.

BROADHURST DRIVE-BY

ICE CUBES
1½ MEASURES GIN
1 MEASURE SWEET VERMOUTH
1 DASH LIME JUICE
1 MEASURE APPLE JUICE
GREEN APPLE SLICE, TO DECORATE
COCKTAIL CHERRY, TO DECORATE

Put some ice cubes into a cocktail shaker with the gin, vermouth and fruit juices and shake to mix. Strain into an old-fashioned glass and decorate with a green apple slice and a cocktail cherry impaled on a cocktail stick.

BRONX

CRACKED ICE, PLUS ICE
CUBES TO SERVE
1 MEASURE GIN
1 MEASURE SWEET
VERMOUTH
1 MEASURE DRY VERMOUTH
2 MEASURES ORANGE JUICE
ORANGE RIND SPIRAL, TO
DECORATE
COCKTAIL CHERRY, TO
DECORATE (OPTIONAL)
MING SPRIG, TO DECORATE

Put some cracked ice into a cocktail shaker and pour the gin, vermouths and orange juice over it. Shake to mix. Strain into an old-fashioned glass over some ice cubes. Decorate with orange slices and a cocktail cherry, if you like.

GINGER TOM

ICE CUBES
1½ MEASURES GIN
1 MEASURE COINTREAU
1 DASH LIME JUICE
1 DASH SWEETENED GINGER
SYRUP
1½ MEASURES CRANBERRY JUICE
LIME RIND SPIRAL, TO DECORATE

Left: Ginger Tom

Put some ice cubes into a cocktail shaker with the gin, Cointreau, lime juice, ginger syrup and cranberry juice and shake to mix. Strain into a chilled cocktail glass and decorate with a lime rind spiral.

PINK GIN

1–4 DASHES ANGOSTURA
BITTERS
1 MEASURE GIN
ICED WATER, TO TOP UP

Shake the bitters into a cocktail glass and swirl them around to coat the inside. Add the gin, then top up with iced water to taste.

HORSE'S NECK

4–6 ICE CUBES
1½ MEASURES GIN
DRY GINGER ALE, TO TOP UP
LEMON RIND SPIRAL, TO DECORATE

Put the ice cubes into a tall glass and pour in the gin. Top up with ginger ale, then dangle the lemon rind spiral over the edge of the glass.

OPERA

4–5 ICE CUBES
1 MEASURE DUBONNET
½ MEASURE CURAÇAO
2 MEASURES GIN
ORANGE RIND SPIRAL, TO DECORATE

Put the ice cubes into a mixing glass. Pour the Dubonnet, Curaçao and gin over the ice. Stir evenly, then strain into a chilled cocktail glass. Decorate with an orange rind spiral.

SYDNEY FIZZ

4–5 ICE CUBES
1 MEASURE LEMON JUICE
1 MEASURE ORANGE JUICE
½ TEASPOON GRENADINE
3 MEASURES GIN
SODA WATER, TO TOP UP
ORANGE SLICE, TO DECORATE

Put the ice cubes into a cocktail shaker. Pour the fruit juices, grenadine and gin over the ice and shake vigorously until a frost forms. Strain into an old-fashioned glass and top up with soda water. Decorate with an orange slice.

FRANKLIN

½ MEASURE DRY VERMOUTH
3 MEASURES ICE-COLD GIN
2 GREEN OLIVES OR LEMON
RIND TWIST, TO DECORATE

Swirl the vermouth around the inside of a chilled Martini glass, then discard the excess. Pour in the ice-cold gin and add the olives (impaled on a cocktail stick) or lemon rind twist.

SAN FRANCISCO

ICE CUBES
1½ MEASURES SLOE GIN
¼ MEASURE SWEET VERMOUTH
¼ MEASURE DRY VERMOUTH
1 DASH ORANGE BITTERS
1 DASH ANGOSTURA BITTERS
COCKTAIL CHERRY, TO DECORATE

Put some ice cubes into a mixing glass. Add the gin, vermouths and bitters and stir well. Pour into a cocktail glass and decorate with a cocktail cherry.

COLLINSON

3 ICE CUBES, CRACKED
1 DASH ORANGE BITTERS
1 MEASURE GIN
½ MEASURE DRY VERMOUTH
¼ MEASURE KIRSCH
LEMON RIND
½ STRAWBERRY, TO DECORATE
LEMON SLICE, TO DECORATE

Put the cracked ice into a mixing glass, then add the bitters, gin, vermouth and kirsch. Stir well and strain into a cocktail glass. Squeeze the zest from the lemon rind over the surface and decorate the rim of the glass with the strawberry half and a lemon slice.

Of all the gin joints in all the towns in all the world, she walks into mine

RICK BLAINE, *CASABLANCA*

WHITE LADY

1 MEASURE GIN
1 MEASURE COINTREAU
1 MEASURE LEMON JUICE
LEMON RIND TWIST, TO
DECORATE (OPTIONAL)

Pour the gin, Cointreau and lemon juice into a cocktail shaker. Shake well, strain into a chilled Martini glass and decorate with a lemon rind twist, if you like.

LADY OF LEISURE

ICE CUBES
1 MEASURE GIN
½ MEASURE CHAMBORD
½ MEASURE COINTREAU
1 DASH LEMON JUICE
1 MEASURE PINEAPPLE JUICE
ORANGE RIND STRIPS, TO
DECORATE
ORANGE SLICE, TO
DECORATE

Put some ice cubes into a cocktail shaker with the gin, Chambord, Cointreau and fruit juices and shake to mix. Strain into a chilled cocktail glass and decorate with an orange rind strip and an orange slice.

GIN AND TONIC

ICE CUBES
2 MEASURES GIN
4 MEASURES TONIC WATER
2 LIME WEDGES, TO DECORATE

Fill a highball glass with ice cubes, pour in the gin and then the tonic water. Decorate with lime wedges.

Right: Gin and Tonic

TANQSTREAM

ICE CUBES, CRACKED
2 MEASURES TANQUERAY GIN
2 TEASPOONS LIME JUICE
3 MEASURES SODA WATER OR
TONIC WATER
2 TEASPOONS CRÈME DE CASSIS
LIME SLICES, TO DECORATE
FRESH BLACKCURRANTS OR
BLUEBERRIES, TO DECORATE
(OPTIONAL)

Put some cracked ice into a cocktail shaker with the gin and lime juice and shake to mix. Strain into a highball glass half-filled with cracked ice. For a dry Tanqstream, add soda water; for a less dry drink, add tonic water. Stir in the créme de cassis and decorate with lime slices and blackcurrants or blueberries, if you like.

ALBEMARLE FIZZ

4–6 ICE CUBES
1 MEASURE TANQUERAY GIN
JUICE OF ½ LEMON
2 DASHES RASPBERRY SYRUP
½ TEASPOON SUGAR SYRUP
SODA WATER, TO TOP UP
COCKTAIL CHERRIES, TO
DECORATE

Put half the ice cubes into a mixing glass and add the gin, lemon juice and raspberry syrup and sugar syrup. Stir to mix, then strain into a highball glass. Add the remaining ice cubes and top up with soda water. Decorate with two cocktail cherries impaled on a cocktail stick and serve with straws.

AVIATION

ICE CUBES
2 MEASURES GIN
½ MEASURE MARASCHINO
LIQUEUR
½ MEASURE LEMON JUICE
COCKTAIL CHERRY, TO
DECORATE

Put some ice cubes into a cocktail shaker with the gin, Maraschino liqueur and lemon juice. Shake well. Double strain into a chilled Martini glass. Decorate with a cocktail cherry impaled on a cocktail stick.

Left: Aviation

FAIR LADY

LIGHTLY BEATEN EGG WHITE
CASTER SUGAR
ICE CUBES
1 MEASURE GIN
4 MEASURES GRAPEFRUIT JUICE
1 DASH COINTREAU

Frost the rim of an old-fashioned glass by dipping it into egg white and pressing it into the sugar. Put some ice cubes into a cocktail shaker and pour the remaining egg white, gin, grapefruit juice and Cointreau over them. Shake well, then pour into the prepared glass.

GOLDEN DAWN

4–5 ICE CUBES
JUICE OF ½ ORANGE
1 MEASURE CALVADOS
1 MEASURE APRICOT BRANDY
3 MEASURES GIN
SODA WATER, TO TOP UP
ORANGE RIND STRIP, TO DECORATE

Put the ice cubes into a cocktail shaker and pour the orange juice, Calvados, apricot brandy and gin over them. Shake until a frost forms. Strain into a highball glass, top up with soda water and decorate with an orange rind strip.

FIGHTING BOB

ICE CUBES
2 MEASURES GIN
½ MEASURE CHARTREUSE
½ MEASURE CHERRY BRANDY
1 TEASPOON LEMON JUICE
1 DASH ANGOSTURA BITTERS
SODA WATER, TO TASTE

Put some ice cubes into a cocktail shaker and pour the gin, Chartreuse, cherry brandy, lemon juice and bitters over them. Shake well, pour into a highball glass or tumbler and add soda water, to taste.

PINK CAMELLIA

ICE CUBES
2 MEASURES GIN
1 MEASURE APRICOT BRANDY
2 MEASURES ORANGE JUICE
2 MEASURES LEMON JUICE
1 MEASURE CAMPARI
1 DASH EGG WHITE

Fill a cocktail shaker three-quarters full with ice cubes. Add all the other ingredients, shake well, then strain into a chilled cocktail glass.

GIN FLORADORA

4–5 ICE CUBES
½ TEASPOON SUGAR SYRUP
JUICE OF ½ LIME
½ TEASPOON GRENADINE
2 MEASURES GIN
DRY GINGER ALE, TO TOP UP
LIME RIND TWIST, TO DECORATE

Put the ice cubes into a cocktail shaker. Pour the sugar syrup, lime juice, grenadine and gin over the ice and shake until a frost forms. Pour without straining into a hurricane glass. Top up with ginger ale and decorate with a lime rind twist.

RIVIERA FIZZ

ICE CUBES
1½ MEASURES SLOE GIN
½ MEASURE LEMON JUICE
½ MEASURE SUGAR SYRUP
CHAMPAGNE, TO TOP UP
LEMON RIND TWIST, TO DECORATE

Put some ice cubes into a cocktail shaker with the sloe gin, lemon juice and sugar syrup and shake well. Strain into a chilled Champagne flute. Top up with Champagne, stir and decorate with a lemon rind twist.

Right: Riviera Fizz

TIPPERARY

4–5 ICE CUBES
JUICE OF 1 LEMON
3 MEASURES GIN
3 MEASURES DRY VERMOUTH

Put the ice cubes into a mixing glass. Pour the lemon juice, gin and vermouth over the ice. Stir evenly and strain into a chilled cocktail glass.

ALICE SPRINGS

4–5 ICE CUBES
1 MEASURE LEMON JUICE
1 MEASURE ORANGE JUICE
½ TEASPOON GRENADINE
3 MEASURES GIN
3 DROPS ANGOSTURA BITTERS
SODA WATER, TO TOP UP
ORANGE SLICE, TO DECORATE

Put the ice cubes into a cocktail shaker. Pour the fruit juices, grenadine and gin over the ice. Add the bitters and shake until a frost forms. Pour into a tall glass and top up with soda water. Decorate with an orange slice and serve with straws.

CHERRY JULEP

3–4 ICE CUBES, PLUS FINELY
CHOPPED ICE TO SERVE
JUICE OF ½ LEMON
1 TEASPOON SUGAR SYRUP
1 TEASPOON GRENADINE
1 MEASURE CHERRY BRANDY
1 MEASURE SLOE GIN
2 MEASURES GIN
LEMON RIND STRIPS, TO
DECORATE

Put the ice cubes into a cocktail shaker. Pour the lemon juice, sugar syrup, grenadine, cherry brandy, gins over the ice. Shake until a frost forms. Strain into a highball glass filled with chopped ice and decorate with lemon rind strips. Serve with a long straw.

BERRY COLLINS

4 RASPBERRIES, PLUS EXTRA TO DECORATE
4 BLUEBERRIES, PLUS EXTRA TO DECORATE
1 DASH STRAWBERRY SYRUP
CRUSHED ICE
2 MEASURES GIN
2 TEASPOONS LEMON JUICE
SUGAR SYRUP, TO TASTE
SODA WATER, TO TOP UP
STRAWBERRY SLICE, TO DECORATE

Muddle the berries and strawberry syrup in a highball glass, then fill the glass with crushed ice. Add the gin, lemon juice and sugar syrup. Stir well, then top up with soda water. Decorate with raspberries, blueberries and a strawberry slice.

Right: Berry Collins

MAIDEN'S BLUSH

ICE CUBES
2 MEASURES GIN
1 MEASURE PERNOD
1 TEASPOON GRENADINE

Put some ice cubes into a cocktail shaker and pour the gin, Pernod and grenadine over them. Shake well and strain into a cocktail glass.

TOM COLLINS

2 MEASURES GIN
1½ TEASPOONS LEMON JUICE
1 TEASPOON SUGAR SYRUP
ICE CUBES
SODA WATER, TO TOP UP
LEMON SLICE, TO DECORATE
COCKTAIL CHERRY, TO
DECORATE

Put the gin, lemon juice and sugar syrup into a tall glass, stir well and fill the glass with ice cubes. Top up with soda water and decorate with a lemon slice and a cocktail cherry.

Right: Tom Collins

MISSISSIPPI MULE

ICE CUBES
1½ MEASURES GIN
1 TEASPOON CRÈME DE CASSIS
1 TEASPOON LEMON JUICE

Put some ice cubes into a cocktail shaker and pour the gin, crème de cassis and lemon juice over them. Shake well, strain into a glass and add more ice cubes.

GIN GARDEN

¼ CUCUMBER, PEELED AND CHOPPED
½ MEASURE ELDERFLOWER CORDIAL
2 MEASURES GIN
1 MEASURE PRESSED APPLE JUICE
ICE CUBES
PEELED CUCUMBER SLICES, TO
DECORATE

Muddle the chopped cucumber and elderflower cordial in a cocktail shaker. Add the gin, apple juice and some ice cubes and shake well. Double strain into a chilled Martini glass and decorate with cucumber slices.

Left: Gin Garden

MAIDEN'S PRAYER

ICE CUBES
2 MEASURES GIN
2 MEASURES COINTREAU
1 MEASURE ORANGE JUICE

Fill a cocktail shaker three-quarters full with ice cubes. Pour the gin, Cointreau and orange juice over the ice and shake well. Strain into a chilled cocktail glass.

POET'S DREAM

4–5 ICE CUBES
1 MEASURE BÉNÉDICTINE
1 MEASURE DRY VERMOUTH
3 MEASURES GIN
LEMON RIND SLICE, TO
DECORATE

Put the ice cubes into a mixing glass. Pour the Bénédictine, vermouth and gin over the ice and stir vigorously, without splashing. Strain into a chilled cocktail glass. Twist the lemon rind slice over the drink, then drop it in.

SINGAPORE SLING

ICE CUBES
1 MEASURE GIN
½ MEASURE CHERRY BRANDY
¼ MEASURE COINTREAU
¼ MEASURE BÉNÉDICTINE
½ MEASURE GRENADINE
½ MEASURE LIME JUICE
5 MEASURES PINEAPPLE JUICE
1 DASH ANGOSTURA BITTERS
PINEAPPLE SLICE, TO DECORATE
COCKTAIL CHERRY, TO DECORATE

Put some ice cubes into a cocktail shaker with all the other ingredients and shake well. Strain into in a sling glass. over the ice cubes Decorate with a pineapple slice and a cocktail cherry impaled on a cocktail stick.

NORTH POLE

1 MEASURE GIN
½ MEASURE LEMON JUICE
½ MEASURE MARASCHINO LIQUEUR
1 EGG WHITE
WHIPPING CREAM, WHIPPED,
TO DECORATE

Put the gin, lemon juice, Maraschino liqueur and egg white into a cocktail shaker and shake well. Pour into a cocktail glass and top with whipped cream.

ZED

CRACKED ICE
1 MEASURE GIN
1 MEASURE MANDARINE
NAPOLÉON BRANDY
3 MEASURES PINEAPPLE JUICE
1 TEASPOON SUGAR
1 LEMON SLICE, CUT IN HALF,
TO DECORATE
MINT SPRIG, TO DECORATE
PINEAPPLE WEDGE, TO
DECORATE
ORANGE RIND STRIPS, TO
DECORATE

Put the cracked ice into a cocktail shaker and pour the gin, Mandarine Napoléon, pineapple juice and sugar over it. Shake lightly to mix. Pour into a tall glass and decorate with the half lemon slices, a mint sprig, a pineapple wedge and orange rind strips.

ORANGE BLOSSOM

4 ORANGE SLICES, PLUS
EXTRA TO DECORATE
2 TEASPOONS ALMOND
SYRUP
CRUSHED ICE
2 MEASURES GIN
1 MEASURE PINK
GRAPEFRUIT JUICE
3 DASHES ANGOSTURA
BITTERS

Muddle the orange slices and almond syrup in a highball glass. Fill the glass with crushed ice and pour in the gin. Stir, top with the grapefruit juice and bitters and decorate with extra orange slices. Serve with straws.

BOXCAR

CASTER SUGAR
ICE CUBES
1¼ MEASURES COINTREAU
1¼ MEASURES GIN
1 TEASPOON LIME JUICE
1 EGG WHITE
1–2 DASHES GRENADINE

Frost the rim of a glass by dipping it into water, then pressing it into the sugar. Put some ice cubes into a cocktail shaker and pour the Cointreau, gin, lime juice, egg white and grenadine over them. Shake very well. Strain into the prepared glass.

WOODSTOCK

Put the crushed ice into a cocktail shaker and add the gin, vermouth, sugar, Cointreau and orange juice. Shake to mix, then strain into a chilled cocktail glass. Squeeze the zest from the orange rind over the surface and decorate with the orange slice twisted over the rim of the glass.

2–3 ICE CUBES, CRUSHED
1 MEASURE GIN
1 MEASURE DRY VERMOUTH
CASTER SUGAR
¼ MEASURE COINTREAU
1 MEASURE ORANGE JUICE
ORANGE RIND
ORANGE SLICE, TO DECORATE

HONG KONG SLING

Put some ice cubes into a cocktail shaker. Pour the gin, lychee liqueur and purée, lemon juice and sugar syrup over them and shake well. Strain over more ice into a sling glass. Stir and top up with soda water. Decorate with a lychee and serve with long straws.

ICE CUBES
1½ MEASURES GIN
½ MEASURE LYCHEE
LIQUEUR
1 MEASURE LYCHEE PURÉE
1 MEASURE LEMON JUICE
½ MEASURE SUGAR SYRUP
SODA WATER, TO TOP UP
FRESH LYCHEE IN ITS
SHELL, TO DECORATE

PERFECT LADY

ICE CUBES
2 MEASURES GIN
1 MEASURE PEACH BRANDY
1 MEASURE LEMON JUICE
1 DASH EGG WHITE

Fill a mixing glass three-quarters full with ice cubes. Add the gin, peach brandy, lemon juice and egg white and stir well. Strain into a chilled cocktail glass.

THE FIX

2 MEASURES GIN
1 DASH PINEAPPLE SYRUP
1 DASH LIME JUICE
1 DASH LEMON JUICE
1 DASH COINTREAU
6–8 ICE CUBES
LEMON RIND, TO DECORATE
PINEAPPLE WEDGES, TO DECORATE

Put the gin, pineapple syrup, fruit juices and Cointreau into a cocktail shaker and shake well. Strain into an old-fashioned glass over the ice cubes and decorate with the lemon rind and pineapple wedges.

KISS IN THE DARK

4–5 ICE CUBES
1 MEASURE GIN
1 MEASURE CHERRY BRANDY
1 TEASPOON DRY VERMOUTH

Put the ice cubes into a cocktail shaker. Pour the gin, cherry brandy and vermouth over them and shake well. Strain into a chilled cocktail glass.

NIGHT OF PASSION

6–8 ICE CUBES
2 MEASURES GIN
1 MEASURE COINTREAU
1 TABLESPOON LEMON JUICE
2 MEASURES PEACH NECTAR
2 TABLESPOONS PASSION FRUIT JUICE

Put half the ice cubes into a cocktail shaker with the gin, Cointreau, lemon juice, peach nectar and passion fruit juice and shake well. Strain into an old-fashioned glass over the remaining ice.

SLOE-HO

2 MEASURES SLOE GIN
1 MEASURE LEMON JUICE
½ MEASURE SUGAR SYRUP
½ MEASURE EGG WHITE
ICE CUBES
SODA WATER, TO TOP UP
LEMON RIND SPIRAL, TO DECORATE

Put the sloe gin, lemon juice, sugar syrup and egg white into a cocktail shaker and shake well. Strain into a highball glass filled with ice cubes and top up with soda water. Decorate with a long lemon rind spiral.

GIN FIZZ

ICE CUBES
2 MEASURES PLYMOUTH GIN
1 MEASURE LEMON JUICE
2–3 DASHES SUGAR SYRUP
¼ EGG WHITE, BEATEN
SODA WATER, TO TOP UP
LEMON SLICES, TO DECORATE
ROSEMARY SPRIG, TO
DECORATE

Put some ice cubes into a cocktail shaker with the gin, lemon juice, sugar syrup and egg white and shake to mix. Strain into a highball glass and top up with soda water. Decorate with lemon slices and a rosemary sprig.

Left: Gin Fizz

VAMPIRE

1 MEASURE DRY VERMOUTH
1 MEASURE GIN
½ MEASURE LIME JUICE

Put all the ingredients into a cocktail shaker and shake well. Pour into a chilled cocktail glass.

ABBEY ROAD

6 MINT LEAVES, PLUS AN EXTRA SPRIG TO DECORATE
1 PIECE CANDIED GINGER
½ MEASURE LEMON JUICE
2 MEASURES GIN
1 MEASURE APPLE JUICE
ICE CUBES, PLUS CRUSHED ICE TO SERVE
LEMON WEDGE, TO DECORATE

Muddle the mint leaves, ginger and lemon juice in a cocktail shaker. Add the gin, apple juice and some ice cubes and shake well. Strain into an old-fashioned glass over crushed ice and decorate with a lemon wedge and a mint sprig. Serve with straws.

Right: Abbey Road

HONEYDEW

3–4 ICE CUBES, CRACKED
1 MEASURE GIN
1/2 MEASURE LEMON JUICE
1 DASH PERNOD
50 G (2 OZ) HONEYDEW MELON, DICED
CHAMPAGNE, TO TOP UP
LEMON RIND STRIPS, TO DECORATE
5 BASIL LEAVES, TO DECORATE

Put the cracked ice, gin, lemon juice, Pernod and melon into a food processor or blender and blend for 30 seconds, then pour into a large wine glass. Top up with Champagne and decorate with lemon rind strips and basil leaves.

Left: Honeydew

CLOVER CLUB

ICE CUBES
JUICE OF 1 LIME
1/2 TEASPOON SUGAR SYRUP
1 EGG WHITE
3 MEASURES GIN
GRATED LIME RIND AND
WEDGE, TO DECORATE

Put some ice cubes into a cocktail shaker. Pour the lime juice, sugar syrup, egg white and gin over them and shake to mix. Strain into an old-fashioned glass over 5–6 more ice cubes. Decorate with grated lime rind and a lime wedge.

I like to have a martini, two at the very most.
After three I'm under the table, after four I'm under my host.
DOROTHY PARKER

SLOE GIN SLING

1 MEASURE SLOE GIN
½ MEASURE LEMON JUICE
SODA WATER, TO TOP UP
LEMON OR ORANGE SLICE, TO
DECORATE
MINT SPRIG, TO DECORATE

Pour the sloe gin and lemon juice into a highball glass. Top up with soda water. Decorate with a lemon or orange slice and a mint sprig.

FRENCH KISS

CRUSHED ICE
1 MEASURE GIN
1 MEASURE DUBONNET
1 MEASURE DRY VERMOUTH
COCKTAIL CHERRY, TO DECORATE

Put some crushed ice into a mixing glass, add the gin, Dubonnet and vermouth and stir well. Strain into a cocktail glass and decorate with a cocktail cherry.

THE DOOBS MARTINI

ICE CUBES
2 TEASPOONS DRY VERMOUTH
2 MEASURES GIN
1 MEASURE SLOE GIN
4 DASHES ORANGE BITTERS
ORANGE RIND TWIST, TO DECORATE
PHYSALIS (CAPE GOOSBERRY), TO DECORATE

Put some ice cubes into a cocktail shaker. Add the vermouth and shake well, then strain away the excess. Add the gins and bitters, stir, then strain into a chilled cocktail glass. Decorate with a physalis and an orange rind twist.

RED LION

ICE CUBES
1½ MEASURES GRAND MARNIER
1 TABLESPOON GIN
2 TEASPOONS ORANGE JUICE
2 TEASPOONS LEMON JUICE
LEMON RIND TWIST, TO
DECORATE

Put some ice cubes into a cocktail shaker and pour the Grand Marnier, gin and fruit juices over them. Shake well and strain into a glass over more ice cubes. Decorate with a lemon rind twist.

FRENCH 75

1 MEASURE GIN
JUICE OF ½ LEMON
1 TEASPOON CASTER
SUGAR
CHILLED CHAMPAGNE, TO
TOP UP
LEMON SLICE, TO
DECORATE

Put the gin, lemon juice and sugar into a Champagne saucer and stir well until the sugar has dissolved. Top up with chilled Champagne and decorate with a lemon slice.

JULIANA BLUE

CRUSHED ICE, PLUS 2–3 ICE
CUBES, TO SERVE
1 MEASURE GIN
½ MEASURE COINTREAU
½ MEASURE BLUE CURAÇAO
2 MEASURES PINEAPPLE JUICE
½ MEASURE LIME JUICE
1 MEASURE COCONUT
CREAM
PINEAPPLE WEDGE, TO
DECORATE
COCKTAIL CHERRIES, TO
DECORATE

Put some crushed ice into a food processor or blender and pour in the gin, Cointreau, blue Curaçao, fruit juices and coconut cream. Blend at high speed for several seconds until the mixture has the consistency of soft snow. Strain into a cocktail glass over ice cubes Decorate with a pineapple wedge and cocktail cherries, impaled on a cocktail stick. Serve with straws.

OPAL MARTINI

ICE CUBES
2 MEASURES GIN
1 MEASURE COINTREAU
2 MEASURES ORANGE
JUICE
ORANGE RIND TWIST, TO
DECORATE

Put some ice cubes into a cocktail shaker with the gin, Cointreau and orange juice and shake well. Strain into a chilled cocktail glass. Swirl a long orange rind twist in the drink and around the stem of the glass.

KNOCKOUT

4–5 ICE CUBES
1 MEASURE DRY VERMOUTH
½ MEASURE WHITE CRÈME DE
MENTHE
2 MEASURES GIN
1 DROP PERNOD
LEMON SLICE, TO DECORATE

Put the ice cubes into a mixing glass. Pour the vermouth, crème de menthe and gin over the ice, stir vigorously, then strain into a chilled old-fashioned glass. Add the Pernod and decorate with a lemon slice.

Do not allow children to mix drinks. It is unseemly and they use too much vermouth.
STEVE ALLEN

RED KISS

Put the cracked ice into a mixing glass, add the vermouth, gin and cherry brandy and stir well. Strain into a chilled cocktail glass and decorate with a cocktail cherry and a lemon rind spiral.

3 ICE CUBES, CRACKED
1 MEASURE DRY VERMOUTH
½ MEASURE GIN
½ MEASURE CHERRY BRANDY
COCKTAIL CHERRY, TO DECORATE
LEMON RIND SPIRAL, TO DECORATE

CROSSBOW

Frost the rim of a chilled cocktail glass by dipping it into water, then pressing it into drinking chocolate powder. Put the ice cubes into a cocktail shaker and add the gin, crème de cacao and Cointreau. Shake vigorously and strain into the prepared glass.

DRINKING CHOCOLATE POWDER
4–5 ICE CUBES
½ MEASURE GIN
½ MEASURE CRÈME DE CACAO
½ MEASURE COINTREAU

LADY OF LEISURE

ICE CUBES
1 MEASURE GIN
½ MEASURE CHAMBORD
½ MEASURE COINTREAU
1 DASH LEMON JUICE
1 MEASURE PINEAPPLE JUICE
ORANGE RIND STRIPS, TO
DECORATE

Put some ice cubes into a cocktail shaker with the gin, Chambord, Cointreau and fruit juices and shake to mix. Strain into a chilled cocktail glass and decorate with orange rind strips.

GIN SLING

4–5 ICE CUBES
JUICE OF ½ LEMON
1 MEASURE CHERRY BRANDY
3 MEASURES GIN
SODA WATER, TO TOP UP

Put the ice cubes into a cocktail shaker. Pour the lemon juice, cherry brandy and gin over the ice. Shake until a frost forms. Pour without straining into a hurricane glass and top up with soda water. Serve with straws.

Right: Gin Sling

VODKA

SEX ON THE BEACH

ICE CUBES
1 MEASURE VODKA
1 MEASURE PEACH SCHNAPPS
1 MEASURE CRANBERRY JUICE
1 MEASURE ORANGE JUICE
1 MEASURE PINEAPPLE JUICE
(OPTIONAL)
ORANGE SLICES, TO DECORATE

Put some ice cubes into a cocktail shaker and add the vodka, schnapps, cranberry juice, orange juice and pineapple juice, if using. Shake well. Pour into a tall glass over 3–4 ice cubes, decorate with the orange and serve with a straw.

Right: Sex on the Beach

ICED LEMON AND MINT VODKA

1 TABLESPOON LEMON JUICE
1 MEASURE LEMON CORDIAL
1 MEASURE CHILLED VODKA
ICE CUBES
TONIC WATER, TO TOP UP
MINT SPRIGS, TO DECORATE

Pour the lemon juice, lemon cordial and vodka into a cocktail shaker and shake well. Pour into a large glass half-filled with ice cubes. Top up with tonic water, add the mint sprigs and serve immediately.

BELLINI-TINI

2 MEASURES VODKA
½ MEASURE PEACH
SCHNAPPS
2 TEASPOONS PEACH JUICE
CHAMPAGNE, TO TOP UP
PEACH SLICES, TO
DECORATE

Put the vodka, schnapps and peach juice into a cocktail shaker and shake well. Pour into a cocktail glass and top up with Champagne. Decorate with peach slices.

WARSAW COCKTAIL

6 ICE CUBES
1 MEASURE VODKA
½ MEASURE BLACKBERRY-
FLAVOURED BRANDY
½ MEASURE DRY
VERMOUTH
1 TEASPOON LEMON
JUICE

Put the ice cubes into a cocktail shaker and add the vodka, brandy, vermouth and lemon juice. Shake until a frost forms. Strain into a cocktail glass.

DIAMOND RING

1 DASH BOILING WATER
1 TEASPOON CLEAR
HONEY
3 BASIL LEAVES
1½ MEASURES ZUBROWKA
BISON GRASS VODKA
1 MEASURE PRESSED
APPLE JUICE
ICE CUBES
APPLE SLICES, TO
DECORATE

Stir the hot water, honey and basil leaves together in a cocktail shaker until well blended. Add the vodka, apple juice and some ice cubes. Shake well and double strain into a chilled Martini glass. Decorate with apple slices.

POLISH MARTINI

ICE CUBES
1 MEASURE ZUBROWKA
VODKA
1 MEASURE KRUPNIK VODKA
1 MEASURE WYBOROWA
VODKA
1 MEASURE APPLE JUICE
LEMON RIND TWIST, TO
DECORATE

Put some ice cubes into a mixing glass. Pour in the vodkas and the apple juice and stir well. Strain into a chilled cocktail glass and add a lemon rind twist.

HARVEY WALLBANGER

ICE CUBES
1 MEASURE VODKA
3 MEASURES ORANGE JUICE
1 TEASPOON GALLIANO
ORANGE SLICES, TO DECORATE

Put some ice cubes into a cocktail shaker and pour the vodka and orange juice over the ice. Shake well for about 10 seconds, then strain into a highball glass filled with ice cubes. Float the Galliano on top. Decorate with orange slices.

MUDSLIDE

10 ICE CUBES, CRACKED
1 MEASURE VODKA
1 MEASURE KAHLÚA
1 MEASURE BAILEYS IRISH CREAM

Put 6 of the cracked ice cubes into a cocktail shaker and add the vodka, Kahlúa and Baileys. Shake until a frost forms. Strain into a tumbler and add the remaining cracked ice.

Cocktail party: A gathering held to enable 40 people to talk about themselves at the same time. The man who remains after the liquor is gone is the host.
FRED ALLEN

MOSCOW MULE

6–8 ICE CUBES, CRACKED
2 MEASURES VODKA
JUICE OF 2 LIMES
GINGER BEER, TO TOP UP
LIME SLICE, TO DECORATE
MINT SPRIG, TO
DECORATE

Put the cracked ice into a highball glass. Add the vodka and lime juice, stir and top up with ginger beer. Decorate with a lime slice and a mint sprig.

NEW DAY

4–5 ICE CUBES
3 MEASURES VODKA
1 MEASURE CALVADOS
1 MEASURE APRICOT BRANDY
JUICE OF ½ ORANGE

Put the ice cubes into a cocktail shaker. Pour the vodka, Calvados, apricot brandy and orange juice over the ice. Shake until a frost forms. Strain into a sour glass.

SCREWDRIVER

2–3 ICE CUBES
1½ MEASURES VODKA
ORANGE JUICE, TO TOP UP
¼ SLICES OF ORANGE, TO
DECORATE

Put the ice cubes into a tumbler and pour the vodka over them. Top up with orange juice and stir lightly. Decorate with orange slice quarters and serve with a straw.

Right: Screwdriver

GINGERSNAP

3 MEASURES VODKA
1 MEASURE GINGER WINE
2–3 ICE CUBES
SODA WATER, TO TOP UP

Combine the vodka, ginger wine and ice cubes in an old-fashioned glass and stir gently. Top up with soda water.

SNAPDRAGON

ICE CUBES
2 MEASURES VODKA
4 MEASURES GREEN CRÈME DE MENTHE
SODA WATER, TO TOP UP
MINT SPRIG, TO DECORATE

Fill a highball glass with ice cubes. Pour the vodka and crème de menthe over the ice and stir. Top up with soda water. Decorate with a mint sprig.

Right: Snapdragon

LAILA COCKTAIL

2 LIME WEDGES
2 STRAWBERRIES, HULLED
4 BLUEBERRIES, PLUS EXTRA TO DECORATE
1 DASH MANGO PURÉE
2 MEASURES RASPBERRY VODKA
ICE CUBES

Muddle the lime wedges, berries and mango purée in a cocktail shaker. Add the vodka with some ice cubes and shake vigorously. Double strain into a chilled Martini glass and garnish with 3 blueberries impaled on a cocktail stick.

SEX IN THE DUNES

ICE CUBES
1 MEASURE VODKA
1 MEASURE PEACH SCHNAPPS
½ MEASURE CHAMBORD
1 MEASURE PINEAPPLE JUICE
PINEAPPLE STRIPS, TO DECORATE

Put some ice cubes into a cocktail shaker with the vodka, schnapps, Chambord and pineapple juice. Shake until a frost forms. Strain into an old-fashioned glass filled with ice cubes. Decorate with pineapple strips.

COSMOPOLITAN

ICE CUBES
1½ MEASURES CITRON VODKA
1 MEASURE COINTREAU
1½ MEASURES CRANBERRY JUICE
¼ MEASURE LIME JUICE
ORANGE RIND TWIST, FLAMED, TO DECORATE

Put ice cubes into a cocktail shaker, add the vodka, Cointreau, and fruit juices and shake well. Strain into a chilled cocktail glass and add a flamed orange rind twist.

RISING SUN

ICE CUBES
2 MEASURES VODKA
2 TEASPOONS PASSION FRUIT SYRUP
3 MEASURES GRAPEFRUIT JUICE
PINK GRAPEFRUIT SLICE, TO
DECORATE

Put some ice cubes into a cocktail shaker with the vodka, passion fruit syrup and grapefruit juice and shake to mix. Strain into an old-fashioned glass over 6–8 ice cubes. Decorate with a pink grapefruit slice.

FLOWER POWER SOUR

ICE CUBES
1½ MEASURES ABSOLUT MANDARIN VODKA
½ MEASURE MANDARINE NAPOLÉON BRANDY
2 TEASPOONS ELDERFLOWER CORDIAL
2 TEASPOONS SUGAR SYRUP
1 MEASURE LEMON JUICE
ORANGE RIND, TO DECORATE

Put some ice cubes into a cocktail shaker with the vodka, Mandarine Napoléon, elderflower cordial, sugar syrup and lemon juice and shake well. Strain into an old-fashioned glass filled with ice cubes and decorate with orange rind.

LEMON MARTINI

ICE CUBES
1½ MEASURES CITRON VODKA
1 MEASURE LEMON JUICE
¼ MEASURE SUGAR SYRUP
¼ MEASURE COINTREAU
3 DROPS ORANGE BITTERS
ORANGE RIND TWIST, TO
DECORATE

Put some ice cubes into a cocktail shaker with the vodka, lemon juice, sugar syrup, Cointreau and bitters and shake well. Strain into a chilled Martini glass and add an orange rind twist.

ILLUSION

4–6 ICE CUBES, PLUS EXTRA TO SERVE
2 MEASURES VODKA
½ MEASURE MIDORI
½ MEASURE TRIPLE SEC
½ MEASURE LIME JUICE
LEMONADE, TO TOP UP
MELON SLICES, TO DECORATE
LEMON SLICES, TO DECORATE
COCKTAIL CHERRY, TO DECORATE

Put the ice cubes into a cocktail shaker with the vodka, Midori, Triple Sec and lime juice and shake well Put more ice cubes into a large hurricane glass and strain the cocktail over the ice. Top up with lemonade, stir and decorate with melon and lemon slices and a cocktail cherry impaled on a cocktail stick. Serve with long straws.

Left: Illusion

ROCK CHICK

ICE CUBES
1 MEASURE ABSOLUT KURANT VODKA
1 DASH PEACH SCHNAPPS
1 DASH LIME JUICE

Put some ice cubes into a cocktail shaker with all the other ingredients and shake briefly. Strain into a shot glass.

SWALLOW DIVE

ICE CUBES, PLUS CRUSHED ICE, TO SERVE
1 MEASURE HONEY VODKA
1 MEASURE CHAMBORD
1 MEASURE LIME JUICE
4 RASPBERRIES, PLUS EXTRA TO DECORATE

Put some ice cubes into a cocktail shaker with all the other ingredients. Shake well. Strain in an old-fashioned glass over crushed ice. Top up with more crushed ice and decorate with the 2 raspberries.

Right: Swallow Dive

OYSTER SHOT

1 SMALL, PLUMP OYSTER
¾ MEASURE CHILLED PEPPER VODKA
¾ MEASURE CHILLED TOMATO JUICE
3 DROPS TABASCO SAUCE
DASH WORCESTERSHIRE SAUCE
1 LIME WEDGE, SQUEEZED
PINCH OF FRESHLY CRACKED BLACK
PEPPER
PINCH OF CELERY SALT

Put all the ingredients into a large shot glass in order, then slowly tip the entire contents down your throat.

Left: Oyster Shot

VODKA GIBSON

6 ICE CUBES
1 MEASURE VODKA
½ MEASURE DRY
VERMOUTH
2 PEARL ONIONS, TO
GARNISH (OPTIONAL)

Put the ice cubes into a cocktail shaker and add the vodka and vermouth. Shake until a frost forms, then strain into a cocktail glass and decorate with 2 pearl onions impaled on a cocktail stick, if you like.

177

TOKYO JOE

ICE CUBES
1 MEASURE VODKA
1 MEASURE MIDORI

Put some ice cubes into a cocktail shaker, add the vodka and Midori and shake well. Strain into an old-fashioned glass, over ice cubes if you like.

VODKATINI

¼ MEASURE DRY VERMOUTH
3 MEASURES VODKA, CHILLED IN THE FREEZER
1 GREEN OLIVE OR LEMON RIND TWIST

Swirl the vermouth around a chilled Martini glass, then pour in the vodka. Finish by adding the olive or a lemon rind twist.

COOL WIND

4–5 ICE CUBES
1 MEASURE DRY VERMOUTH
½ TEASPOON COINTREAU
3 MEASURES VODKA
JUICE OF ½ GRAPEFRUIT

Put the ice cubes into a mixing glass. Pour the vermouth, Cointreau, vodka and grapefruit juice over the ice. Stir gently, then strain into a chilled cocktail glass.

DRAGON'S FIRE

ICE CUBES
1½ MEASURES ABSOLUT
MANDARIN VODKA
1 MEASURE COINTREAU
1 DASH LIME JUICE
1 MEASURE CRANBERRY JUICE
ORANGE RIND TWIST, TO
DECORATE

Put some ice cubes into a cocktail shaker with the vodka, Cointreau and fruit juices and shake well. Double strain into a chilled Martini glass. Decorate with an orange rind twist.

FRENCH LEAVE

ICE CUBES
1 MEASURE ORANGE JUICE
1 MEASURE VODKA
1 MEASURE PERNOD

Put some ice cubes into a cocktail shaker with all the other ingredients and shake well. Strain into a cocktail glass.

LEMON DROP

ICE CUBES
3/4 MEASURE LEMON VODKA
3/4 MEASURE LIMONCELLO
1 DASH LEMON JUICE
1 DASH LIME CORDIAL
TOMATO WEDGE, TO
DECORATE

Put some ice cubes into a cocktail shaker with all the other ingredients and shake briefly. Strain into a shot glass and decorate with a tomato wedge.

Right: Lemon Drop

STORM AT SEA

8–10 ICE CUBES
2 MEASURES CRANBERRY JUICE
1 MEASURE PINEAPPLE JUICE
2 TEASPOONS ELDERFLOWER
CORDIAL
1½ MEASURES BLAVOD VODKA

Put half the ice cubes into a cocktail shaker with the fruit juices and elderflower cordial and shake well. Strain into an old-fashioned glass over the remaining ice cubes. Slowly add the vodka – it will separate briefly. Serve immediately.

PLASMA

ICE CUBES
2 MEASURES ABSOLUT PEPPAR VODKA
4 MEASURES TOMATO JUICE
JUICE OF ¼ LEMON
2 DASHES TABASCO SAUCE
4 DASHES WORCESTERSHIRE SAUCE
PINCH OF CELERY SALT
PINCH OF BLACK PEPPER
½ TEASPOON DIJON MUSTARD
1 TEASPOON FINELY CHOPPED DILL
LEMON SLICE, TO DECORATE
PARSLEY SPRIG, TO DECORATE

Put some ice cubes into a cocktail shaker with all the other ingredients. Shake vigorously but briefly, then strain into a highball glass over 6–8 ice cubes. Decorate with a lemon slice and a parsley sprig.

May your glass be ever full. May the roof over your head be always strong. And may you be in heaven half an hour before the devil knows you're dead.
IRISH DRINKING TOAST

Left: Plasma

WHITE SPIDER

2 MEASURES VODKA
1 MEASURE CLEAR CRÈME
DE MENTHE
CRUSHED ICE (OPTIONAL)

Pour the vodka and crème de menthe into a cocktail shaker. Shake well, then pour into a cocktail glass, chilled, or over crushed ice.

XANTIPPE

4–5 ICE CUBES
1 MEASURE CHERRY BRANDY
1 MEASURE YELLOW
CHARTREUSE
2 MEASURES VODKA

Put the ice cubes into a mixing glass. Pour the cherry brandy, Chartreuse and vodka over the ice and stir vigorously. Strain into a chilled cocktail glass.

CHOCOTINI

COCOA POWDER
ICE CUBES
2 MEASURES VODKA
1 MEASURE DARK CRÈME DE CACAO
¼ MEASURE SUGAR SYRUP
½ MEASURE CHOCOLATE SYRUP

Frost the rim of a chilled Martini glass by dipping it in water, then pressing it into cocoa powder. Put some ice cubes into a cocktail shaker, add the vodka, crème de cacao, sugar syrup and chocolate syrup and shake well. Strain into the prepared glass.

WHITE RUSSIAN

6 ICE CUBES, CRACKED
1 MEASURE VODKA
1 MEASURE TIA MARIA
1 MEASURE MILK OR
DOUBLE CREAM

Put half the cracked ice into a cocktail shaker and add the vodka, Tia Maria and milk or cream. Shake until a frost forms. Strain into a tall, narrow glass over the remaining ice cubes.

MURRAY HEARN

ICE CUBES
1½ MEASURES VODKA
3 MEASURES ORANGE JUICE
½ MEASURE GALLIANO
½ MEASURE COINTREAU
1 MEASURE SINGLE CREAM
ORANGE SLICE, TO DECORATE

Put some ice cubes into a cocktail shaker and add the vodka, orange juice, Galliano, Cointreau and cream. Shake well, then strain into a highball glass filled with ice cubes. Decorate with an orange slice.

FRAGRANCE

4–6 ICE CUBES, PLUS CRUSHED ICE, TO SERVE
1½ MEASURES VODKA
½ MEASURE MIDORI
1 MEASURE LEMON JUICE
1 MEASURE PINEAPPLE JUICE
1 DASH SUGAR SYRUP
1 LEMON WEDGE

Put the ice cubes into a cocktail shaker with the vodka, Midori, fruit juices and sugar syrup and shake. Strain into a highball glass filled with crushed ice. Squeeze the lemon wedge over the surface, drop it in and serve with straws.

Right: Fragrance

ONE OF THOSE

1 MEASURE VODKA
4 MEASURES CRANBERRY JUICE
2 DASHES AMARETTO DI SARONNO
LIQUEUR
JUICE OF ½ LIME
ICE CUBES
LIME SLICE, TO DECORATE

Pour the vodka, cranberry juice, Amaretto di Saronno and lime juice into a cocktail shaker and shake well. Pour into a highball glass half-filled with ice cubes and decorate with a lime slice.

WATERMELON MARTINI

1 LIME WEDGE
ICE CUBES
4 WATERMELON CHUNKS
1½ MEASURES VODKA
½ MEASURE PASSION FRUIT
LIQUEUR
1 DASH CRANBERRY JUICE
WATERMELON WEDGE, TO
DECORATE

Squeeze the lime wedge into a cocktail shaker, add some ice cubes, the watermelon chunks, vodka, passion fruit liqueur and cranberry juice and shake well. Double strain into a chilled Martini glass and decorate with a watermelon wedge on the edge of the glass.

Left: Watermelon Martini

GODMOTHER

2–3 ICE CUBES, CRACKED
1½ MEASURES VODKA
½ MEASURE AMARETTO DI SARONNO
LIQUEUR

Put the cracked ice into a tumbler. Add the vodka and Amaretto di Saronno and stir lightly.

APPLE MARTINI

ICE CUBES
2 MEASURES VODKA
1 MEASURE APPLE SCHNAPPS
1 TABLESPOON APPLE PURÉE
1 DASH LIME JUICE
PINCH OF GROUND CINNAMON
APPLE WEDGES, TO DECORATE

Put some ice cubes into a cocktail shaker with the vodka, schnapps, apple purée, lime juice and cinnamon and shake well. Double strain into a chilled Martini glass. Decorate with apple wedges.

Right: Apple Martini

CAPE CODDER

ICE CUBES
2 MEASURES VODKA
4 MEASURES CRANBERRY JUICE
LIME SLICE, TO DECORATE

Fill a highball glass with ice cubes. Pour the vodka and cranberry juice over the ice. Squeeze the lime wedges into the drink. Stir well, decorate with a lime slice and serve with straws.

Right: Cape Codder

DARK KNIGHT

ICE CUBES
1 MEASURE KAHLÚA
1 MEASURE VODKA
1 MEASURE COLD ESPRESSO COFFEE
2 TEASPOONS SUGAR SYRUP

Put some ice cubes into a cocktail shaker with the Kahlúa, vodka, coffee and sugar syrup and shake well. Strain into a chilled Martini glass.

Beer is not a good cocktail-party drink, especially in a home where you don't know where the bathroom is.
BILLY CARTER

PDQ

4–5 ICE CUBES
1½ MEASURES CHILLI-FLAVOURED VODKA
1 MEASURE VODKA
2 MEASURES CHILLED BEEF STOCK
1 TABLESPOON LEMON JUICE
1 DASH TABASCO SAUCE
1 DASH WORCESTERSHIRE SAUCE
SALT AND BLACK PEPPER
LEMON SLICE, TO DECORATE
CHILLI, TO DECORATE

Put the ice cubes into a cocktail shaker. Pour the vodkas, stock, lemon juice and Tabasco and Worcestershire sauces over the ice. Shake until a frost forms. Strain into a hurricane glass. Season to taste with salt and pepper and decorate with a lemon slice and a chilli.

KURANT BLUSH

ICE CUBES
1½ MEASURES ABSOLUT KURANT VODKA
½ MEASURE FRAISE LIQUEUR
1 MEASURE CRANBERRY JUICE
2 LIME WEDGES
REDCURRANT STRING, TO DECORATE
ORANGE RIND SPIRAL, TO DECORATE

Put some ice cubes into a cocktail shaker with all the other ingredients and shake well. Double strain into a chilled Martini glass and decorate with a redcurrant string and an orange rind spiral.

KATINKA

ICE CUBES
1½ MEASURES VODKA
1 MEASURE APRICOT BRANDY
2 TEASPOONS LIME JUICE
MINT SPRIG, TO DECORATE

Put some ice cubes into a cocktail shaker with all the other ingredients and shake well. Strain into a cocktail glass and decorate with a mint sprig.

DECATINI

ICE CUBES
2 MEASURES RASPBERRY VODKA
½ MEASURE CHOCOLATE SYRUP, PLUS
EXTRA TO DECORATE
½ MEASURE DOUBLE CREAM
1 MEASURE MORELLO CHERRY PURÉE

Fill a cocktail shaker with ice cubes and add the vodka, chocolate syrup and half the cream. Shake well and strain into a chilled Martini glass. Shake the morello cherry purée with the remaining cream in a clean cocktail shaker. Slowly pour the cherry liquid onto a spoon that is held in contact with the chocolate liquid in the glass; this will produce a layering effect. Decorate with a 'swirl' of chocolate syrup.

LE MANS

2–3 ICE CUBES, CRACKED
1 MEASURE COINTREAU
½ MEASURE VODKA
SODA WATER, TO TOP UP
LEMON SLICE, TO DECORATE

Put the cracked ice into a tall glass. Add the Cointreau and vodka, stir and top up with soda water. Float a lemon slice on top of the drink for decoration.

SEA BREEZE

ICE CUBES
2 MEASURES VODKA
4 MEASURES CRANBERRY JUICE
2 MEASURES PINK GRAPEFRUIT JUICE
2 LIME WEDGES

Fill a highball glass with ice cubes. Pour the vodka and fruit juices over the ice. Squeeze the lime wedges over the drink, then drop them in and stir lightly. Serve with straws.

ICEBERG

4–6 ICE CUBES
1½ MEASURES VODKA
1 DASH PERNOD

Put the ice cubes into an old-fashioned glass. Pour the vodka over the ice and add the Pernod.

ASTRONAUT

8–10 ICE CUBES, CRACKED
½ MEASURE WHITE RUM
½ MEASURE VODKA
½ MEASURE LEMON JUICE
1 DASH PASSION FRUIT JUICE
LEMON WEDGE, TO
DECORATE

Put half the cracked ice into a cocktail shaker and add the rum, vodka and fruit juices. Shake until a frost forms. Strain into an old-fashioned glass filled with the remaining ice cubes. Decorate with a lemon wedge.

YOKOHAMA

4–5 ICE CUBES
3 MEASURES VODKA
3 DROPS PERNOD
JUICE OF 1 ORANGE
½ TEASPOON GRENADINE
ORANGE WEDGES, TO
DECORATE

Put the ice cubes into a cocktail shaker. Pour the vodka, Pernod, orange juice and grenadine over the ice. Shake until a frost forms. Strain into a chilled cocktail glass. Decorate with orange wedges and serve with straws.

VODKA SAZERAC

1 SUGAR CUBE
2 DROPS ANGOSTURA
BITTERS
3 DROPS PERNOD
2–3 ICE CUBES
2 MEASURES VODKA
LEMONADE, TO TOP UP

Put the sugar cube into an old-fashioned glass and shake the bitters onto it. Add the Pernod and swirl it around to coat the inside of the glass. Drop in the ice cubes and pour in the vodka. Top up with lemonade and stir gently.

BLUE MOON

5–6 ICE CUBES, CRACKED
¾ MEASURE VODKA
¾ MEASURE TEQUILA
1 MEASURE BLUE CURAÇAO
LEMONADE, TO TOP UP

Put half the cracked ice into a mixing glass. Add the vodka, tequila and Curaçao and stir to mix. Strain into a tall glass over the remaining cracked ice. Top up with lemonade and serve with a straw.

BASIL'S MANGO SLING

ICE CUBES, PLUS CRUSHED
ICE, TO SERVE
1½ MEASURES VODKA
1½ MEASURES MANGO PURÉE
1 MEASURE APRICOT LIQUEUR
½ MEASURE LEMON JUICE
1 DASH SUGAR SYRUP
SODA WATER, TO TOP UP
MANGO SLICES, TO
DECORATE

Put some ice cubes into a cocktail shaker with the vodka, mango purée, apricot liqueur, lemon juice and sugar syrup and shake very briefly. Strain into a sling glass filled with crushed ice. Top up with soda water and decorate with mango slices.

HAIR RAISER

1–2 ICE CUBES, CRACKED
1 MEASURE VODKA
1 MEASURE SWEET VERMOUTH
1 MEASURE TONIC WATER
LEMON AND LIME RIND SPIRALS, TO
DECORATE

Put the cracked ice into a tall glass and pour the vodka, vermouth and tonic water over it. Stir lightly. Decorate with the lemon and lime rind spirals and serve with a straw.

PILLOW TALK

½ MEASURE CHILLED STRAWBERRY VODKA
½ MEASURE MOZART WHITE CHOCOLATE
LIQUEUR
1 DASH AEROSOL CREAM

Pour the chilled vodka into a shot glass. Using the back of a bar spoon, slowly float the chocolate liqueur over the vodka. Top with the cream.

VODKA COLLINS

6 ICE CUBES
2 MEASURES VODKA
JUICE OF 1 LIME
1 TEASPOON CASTER SUGAR
SODA WATER, TO TOP UP
LEMON OR LIME SLICE, TO DECORATE
COCKTAIL CHERRY, TO DECORATE

Put half of the ice cubes into a cocktail shaker and add the vodka, lime juice and sugar. Shake until a frost forms. Strain into a large tumbler; add the remaining ice and top up with soda water. Decorate with a slice of lemon or lime and a cocktail cherry.

HAVEN

2–3 ICE CUBES
1 TABLESPOON GRENADINE
1 MEASURE PERNOD
1 MEASURE VODKA
SODA WATER, TO TOP UP
ORANGES SLICE, TO
DECORATE

Put the ice cubes into an old-fashioned glass. Dash the grenadine over the ice, then pour in the Pernod and vodka. Top up with soda water and decorate with an orange slice.

MACHETE

ICE CUBES
1 MEASURE VODKA
2 MEASURES PINEAPPLE JUICE
3 MEASURES TONIC WATER

Fill a tall glass or wine glass with ice cubes. Pour the vodka, pineapple juice and tonic water into a mixing glass. Stir, then pour the mixture over the ice cubes in the glass.

VOCACHINO

ICE CUBES
2 MEASURES VODKA
½ MEASURE KAHLÚA
½ MEASURE COLD
ESPRESSO COFFEE
½ MEASURE SINGLE CREAM
1 DASH SUGAR SYRUP
½ TEASPOON COCOA
POWDER

Put some ice cubes into a cocktail shaker and add the vodka, Kahlúa, coffee, cream, sugar syrup and cocoa powder. Shake briefly then strain into shot glasses. Serves 4.

Right: Vocachino

PURPLE HAZE

ICE CUBES
1 MEASURE VODKA
1 DASH COINTREAU
1 DASH LEMON JUICE
1 DASH CHAMBORD

Put some ice cubes into a cocktail shaker with the vodka, Cointreau and lemon juice and shake briefly. Strain into a shot glass. Add the dash of Chambord slowly at the end: this will settle towards the bottom of the drink.

Right: Purple Haze

MARGUERITE

4–5 ICE CUBES, PLUS CRACKED ICE,
TO SERVE
3 MEASURES VODKA
JUICE OF 1 LEMON
JUICE OF ½ ORANGE
RASPBERRY SYRUP, MARASCHINO
LIQUEUR OR GRENADINE, TO TASTE

Put the ice cubes into a cocktail shaker. Pour the vodka, fruit juices and raspberry syrup, Maraschino liqueur or grenadine over the ice. Shake until a frost forms. Strain into an old-fashioned glass filled with cracked ice.

> The whole world is drunk and we're just the cocktail of the moment. Someday soon, the world will wake up, down two aspirin with a glass of tomato juice, and wonder what the hell all the fuss was about.
> **DEAN MARTIN, *THE RAT PACK***

COMBINED FORCES

4–5 ICE CUBES
2 MEASURES VODKA
1 MEASURE DRY
VERMOUTH
½ TEASPOON TRIPLE SEC
JUICE OF ½ FRESH LEMON

Put the ice cubes into a mixing glass. Add all the other ingredients, stir vigorously then strain into a chilled cocktail glass.

WHITE LEOPARD

4–5 ICE CUBES
2 MEASURES VODKA
1 MEASURE GRAND MARNIER
JUICE OF ½ ORANGE
JUICE OF ½ LEMON

Put the ice cubes into a cocktail shaker. Pour the vodka, Grand Marnier and fruit juices over the ice. Shake until a frost forms. Strain into a sour glass.

INSPIRATION

4–5 ICE CUBES
½ MEASURE BÉNÉDICTINE
½ MEASURE DRY VERMOUTH
2 MEASURES VODKA
LIME RIND SPIRAL, TO DECORATE

Put the ice cubes into a mixing glass. Pour the Bénédictine, vermouth and vodka over the ice. Stir vigorously, then strain into a chilled cocktail glass and decorate with the lime rind spiral.

LEMON GRASS COLLINS

CRUSHED ICE
2 MEASURES LEMON GRASS VODKA
½ MEASURE VANILLA LIQUEUR
1 DASH LEMON JUICE
1 DASH SUGAR SYRUP
GINGER BEER, TO TOP UP
LEMON SLICES, TO DECORATE

Fill a large Collins glass with crushed ice. Pour, in order, the vodka, vanilla liqueur, lemon juice and sugar syrup over the ice. Stir, add more crushed ice and top up with ginger beer. Decorate with lemon slices and serve with long straws.

GREEN ISLAND QUIET SUNDAY

4–6 ICE CUBES, PLUS CRUSHED ICE, TO
SERVE
1 MEASURE VODKA
4 MEASURES ORANGE JUICE
3 DASHES AMARETTO DI SARONNO
LIQUEUR
FEW DROPS GRENADINE

Put the ice cubes into a cocktail shaker with the vodka, orange juice and Amaretto di Saronno and shake well. Strain into a highball glass filled with crushed ice. Add a few drops of grenadine.

BAY BREEZE

ICE CUBES
4 MEASURES CRANBERRY JUICE
2 MEASURES VODKA
2 MEASURES PINEAPPLE JUICE
LIME WEDGES, TO DECORATE

Fill a highball glass with ice cubes and pour in the cranberry juice. Pour the vodka and pineapple juice into a chilled cocktail shaker. Shake well, then pour gently over the cranberry juice. Decorate with lime wedges and serve with long straws.

Left: Bay Breeze

STRAWBERRY FIELDS

1 LIME WEDGE
1 DASH STRAWBERRY SYRUP
1 STRAWBERRY, HULLED
1 MEASURE ABSOLUT KURANT
VODKA
ICE CUBES

Muddle the lime wedge, strawberry syrup and strawberry in a cocktail shaker, add the vodka and some ice cubes and shake briefly. Strain into a shot glass.

Right: Strawberry Fields

BLOODY MARY

4–5 ICE CUBES
JUICE OF ½ LEMON
½ TEASPOON
HORSERADISH SAUCE
2 DROPS
WORCESTERSHIRE SAUCE
1 DROP TABASCO SAUCE
2 MEASURES THICK
TOMATO JUICE
2 MEASURES VODKA
PINCH OF SALT
PINCH OF CAYENNE
PEPPER
CELERY STICK, WITH
THE LEAVES LEFT ON, TO
DECORATE
LEMON SLICE, TO
DECORATE
GREEN OLIVES, TO
DECORATE

Put the ice cubes into a cocktail shaker. Pour the lemon juice, horseradish, Worcestershire and Tabasco sauces, tomato juice and vodka over the ice. Shake until a frost forms. Pour into a tall glass and add the salt and cayenne pepper. Decorate with a celery stick, lemon slice and 3 olives.

BLACK RUSSIAN

CRACKED ICE
2 MEASURES VODKA
1 MEASURE KAHLÚA
CHOCOLATE STICK, TO DECORATE
(OPTIONAL)

Put some cracked ice into a mixing glass. Add the vodka and Kahlúa and stir. Pour into a short glass without straining. Decorate with a chocolate stick, if you like. Serve with a straw.

Left: Black Russian

ROAD RUNNER

6 ICE CUBES, CRACKED
2 MEASURES VODKA
1 MEASURE AMARETTO DI
SARONNO LIQUEUR
1 MEASURE COCONUT MILK
GRATED NUTMEG, TO
DECORATE

Put the cracked ice into a cocktail shaker and add the vodka, Amaretto di Saronno and coconut milk. Shake until a frost forms, then strain into a cocktail glass. Sprinkle with a pinch of freshly grated nutmeg.

VODKA SOUR

4–5 ICE CUBES
2 MEASURES VODKA
1/2 MEASURE SUGAR SYRUP
1 EGG WHITE
1 1/2 MEASURES LEMON
JUICE
3 DROPS ANGOSTURA
BITTERS, TO DECORATE

Put the ice cubes into a cocktail shaker, add the vodka, sugar syrup, egg white and lemon juice and shake until a frost forms. Pour without straining into a cocktail glass and shake the Angostura bitters on the top to decorate.

THE GLAMOUR MARTINI

ICE CUBES
1 1/2 MEASURES VODKA
1/2 MEASURE CHERRY
BRANDY
2 MEASURES BLOOD
ORANGE JUICE
1/2 MEASURE LIME JUICE
ORANGE RIND TWIST, TO
DECORATE

Put some ice cubes into a cocktail shaker with all the other ingredients and shake well. Strain into a chilled Martini glass. Decorate with an orange rind twist and serve with a straw.

SURF RIDER

4–5 ICE CUBES
3 MEASURES VODKA
1 MEASURE SWEET VERMOUTH
JUICE OF ½ LEMON
JUICE OF 1 ORANGE
½ TEASPOON GRENADINE

Put the ice cubes into a cocktail shaker. Pour the vodka, vermouth, fruit juices and grenadine over the ice. Shake until a frost forms. Strain into a sour glass.

VESPER

ICE CUBES
3 MEASURES GIN
1 MEASURE VODKA
½ MEASURE LILLET APÉRITIF WINE
LEMON RIND TWIST, TO DECORATE

Put some ice cubes into a cocktail shaker with the gin, vodka and Lillet and shake well. Strain into a chilled cocktail glass and add a lemon rind twist.

VALENTINE MARTINI

ICE CUBES
2 MEASURES RASPBERRY
VODKA
6 RASPBERRIES, PLUS
EXTRA TO DECORATE
½ MEASURE LIME JUICE
1 DASH SUGAR SYRUP
LIME RIND TWIST, TO
DECORATE

Put some ice cubes into a cocktail shaker with the vodka, raspberries, lime juice and sugar syrup and shake well. Double strain into a chilled Martini glass. Decorate with 2 raspberries impaled on a cocktail stick and a lime rind twist.

RAZZMOPOLITAN

1½ MEASURES
STOLICHNAYA RAZBERI
VODKA
1 MEASURE COINTREAU
1 DASH LIME JUICE
1 MEASURE CRANBERRY
JUICE
4 RASPBERRIES, PLUS
EXTRA TO DECORATE

Put the vodka, Cointreau, fruit juices and raspberries into a cocktail shaker and shake well. Double strain into a chilled Martini glass and decorate with 2 raspberries impaled on a cocktail stick.

LEGAL HIGH

1 DASH AMARETTO DI SARONNO
LIQUEUR
1 PINK GRAPEFRUIT WEDGE
1 MEASURE VODKA (HEMP VODKA)
ICE CUBES

Muddle the Amaretto di Saronno and grapefruit in the base of a cocktail shaker. Add the vodka and a few ice cubes and shake briefly. Strain into a shot glass.

OCTOBER REVOLUTION

5–6 ICE CUBES, CRACKED
1 MEASURE VODKA
1 MEASURE TIA MARIA
1 MEASURE CRÈME DE CACAO
1 MEASURE DOUBLE CREAM

Put half the cracked ice into a cocktail shaker. Pour the vodka, Tia Maria, crème de cacao and cream over the ice and shake until a frost forms. Strain into a tall, narrow glass over the remaining cracked ice and serve with a straw.

BLACKBERRY MARTINI

2 MEASURES ABSOLUT KURANT VODKA
1 MEASURE CRÈME DE MURE
ICE CUBES
BLACKBERRY, TO DECORATE

Put the vodka and crème de mure into a mixing glass, add some ice cubes and stir well. Strain into a chilled Martini glass and decorate with a single blackberry impaled on a cocktail stick.

MELON BALL

5 ICE CUBES, CRACKED
1 MEASURE VODKA
1 MEASURE MIDORI
1 MEASURE ORANGE JUICE, PLUS EXTRA FOR TOPPING UP (OPTIONAL)
ORANGE SLICE, TO DECORATE
BANANA BALL, TO DECORATE

Put the cracked ice into a tall glass or goblet. Pour the vodka, Midori and orange juice into a cocktail shaker. Shake well, then strain into the glass. Top up with more orange juice, if necessary. Decorate with an orange slice and a banana ball and serve with a straw.

Let us candidly admit that there are shameful blemishes on the American past, of which the worst by far is rum. Nevertheless, we have improved man's lot and enriched his civilization with rye, bourbon and the Martini cocktail. In all history has any other nation done so much?

BERNARD DE VOTO

PARROT'S HEAD PUNCH

ICE CUBES
1 1/2 MEASURES VODKA
1 MEASURE PASSION FRUIT
LIQUEUR
2 MEASURES WATERMELON
JUICE
1 MEASURE CRANBERRY JUICE
1 1/2 MEASURES PINK
GRAPEFRUIT JUICE
GRAPEFRUIT SLICES, TO
DECORATE

Fill a hurricane glass with ice cubes. Pour all the other ingredients, one by one in order, over the ice. Decorate with grapefruit slices and serve with long straws.

WHISKEY

RHETT BUTLER

4–5 ICE CUBES, PLUS EXTRA TO SERVE
2 MEASURES BOURBON WHISKEY
4 MEASURES CRANBERRY JUICE
2 TABLESPOONS SUGAR SYRUP
1 TABLESPOON LIME JUICE
LIME SLICES, TO DECORATE

Put the ice cubes into a cocktail shaker with the bourbon, cranberry juice, sugar syrup and lime juice and shake well. Strain an old-fashioned glass filled with with ice cubes. Decorate with lime slices and serve with straws.

BIG BUFF

1 STRAWBERRY, HULLED
3 RASPBERRIES
3 BLUEBERRIES, PLUS
EXTRA TO DECORATE
2 TEASPOONS CHAMBORD
1 DASH LIME JUICE
2 MEASURES BUFFALO
TRACE BOURBON WHISKEY
3 MEASURES CRANBERRY
JUICE
4–5 ICE CUBES

Muddle the berries and Chambord in a cocktail shaker. Add the lime juice, bourbon, cranberry juice and ice cubes. Shake, then pour without straining into a highball glass and decorate with blueberries.

BOURBON FIXED

ICE CUBES
2 MEASURES BOURBON
WHISKEY
1 MEASURE MORELLO
CHERRY PURÉE
1 TABLESPOON LIME JUICE
2 TEASPOONS SUGAR
SYRUP
LIME RIND SPIRALS, TO
DECORATE
2 CHERRIES, TO DECORATE

Put some ice cubes into a cocktail shaker with the bourbon, cherry purée, lime juice and sugar syrup and shake to mix. Strain into an old-fashioned glass filled with ice cubes and decorate with lime rind spirals and 2 cherries impaled on a cocktail stick.

CAPRICORN

4–5 ICE CUBES, CRACKED
1 MEASURE BOURBON
WHISKEY
½ MEASURE APRICOT BRANDY
½ MEASURE LEMON JUICE
2 MEASURES ORANGE JUICE
ORANGE SLICE, TO
DECORATE

Put half the cracked ice into a cocktail shaker and add the bourbon, apricot brandy and fruit juices. Shake to mix. Strain into an old-fashioned glass over the remaining cracked ice. Decorate with an orange slice.

RICKEY

4–5 ICE CUBES
1½ MEASURES BOURBON WHISKEY
1½ MEASURES LIME JUICE
SODA WATER, TO TOP UP
LIME RIND TWIST, TO DECORATE

Put the ice cubes into a tall glass with the bourbon and lime juice. Top up with soda water and stir. Garnish with a lime rind twist.

TAR

4–5 ICE CUBES
JUICE OF 1 LEMON
½ TEASPOON GRENADINE
1 MEASURE CRÈME DE CACAO
3 MEASURES SCOTCH WHISKY

Put the ice cubes into a cocktail shaker. Pour in the lemon juice, grenadine, crème de cacao and whisky and shake until a frost forms. Strain into a chilled cocktail glass. Serve with a straw.

BENEDICT

3–4 ICE CUBES
1 MEASURE BÉNÉDICTINE
3 MEASURES SCOTCH
WHISKY
DRY GINGER ALE, TO
TOP UP
LEMON WEDGE, TO
DECORATE

Put the ice cubes into a mixing glass. Pour the Bénédictine and whisky over the ice. Stir evenly without splashing. Pour without straining into a chilled highball glass. Top up with ginger ale and decorate with a lemon wedge.

MINT JULEP I

10 MINT LEAVES, PLUS AN
EXTRA SPRIG, TO DECORATE
1 TEASPOON SUGAR SYRUP
4 DASHES ANGOSTURA BITTERS
CRUSHED ICE
2 MEASURES BOURBON
WHISKEY

Muddle the mint leaves, sugar syrup and bitters in a highball glass. Fill the glass with crushed ice, then add the bourbon. Stir well and decorate with a mint sprig. Serve with a long straw.

Right: Mint Julep I

MINT JULEP II

3 SPRIGS MINT, PLUS EXTRA TO
DECORATE
½ TABLESPOON CASTER SUGAR
1 TABLESPOON SODA WATER
2–3 ICE CUBES
1 MEASURE BOURBON WHISKEY

Crush the mint with the sugar in an old-fashioned glass or large tumbler and rub it around the insides of the glass. Discard the mint. Dissolve the sugar in the soda water, add the ice cubes and pour the bourbon over it. Do not stir. Decorate with the extra mint sprig.

CLIQUET

4–5 ICE CUBES
JUICE OF 1 ORANGE
3 MEASURES BOURBON
WHISKEY OR SCOTCH
WHISKY
1 TABLESPOON DARK RUM
ORANGE RIND TWIST, TO
DECORATE

Put the ice cubes into a mixing glass. Pour the orange juice, bourbon or whisky and rum over the ice. Stir vigorously, then strain into a sour glass. Decorate with an orange rind twist.

ALGONQUIN

4–5 ICE CUBES
1 MEASURE PINEAPPLE JUICE
1 MEASURE DRY VERMOUTH
3 MEASURES BOURBON WHISKEY
OR SCOTCH WHISKY

Put the ice cubes into a mixing glass. Pour the pineapple juice, vermouth and bourbon or whisky over the ice. Stir vigorously until nearly frothy, then strain into a chilled cocktail glass. Serve with a straw.

Always do sober what you said you'd do drunk.
That will teach you to keep your mouth shut
ERNEST HEMINGWAY

WHIZZ BANG

4–5 ICE CUBES
3 DROPS ORANGE BITTERS
½ TEASPOON GRENADINE
1 MEASURE DRY VERMOUTH
3 MEASURES SCOTCH WHISKY
1 DROP PERNOD

Put the ice cubes into a mixing glass. Shake the bitters over the ice and pour in the grenadine, vermouth and whisky. Stir vigorously, then strain into a chilled cocktail glass. Add the Pernod and stir.

VIRGINIA MINT JULEP

9 YOUNG MINT SPRIGS, PLUS EXTRA TO DECORATE
1 TEASPOON SUGAR SYRUP
CRUSHED ICE
3 MEASURES BOURBON WHISKEY

Muddle the mint and sugar syrup in an iced silver mug or tall glass. Fill the mug or glass with crushed ice, pour the bourbon over the ice and stir gently. Pack in more crushed ice and stir until a frost forms. Wrap the mug or glass in a table napkin and decorate with a mint sprig.

EARLY NIGHT

1 TABLESPOON LEMON JUICE
1 MEASURE CLEAR HONEY
1 MEASURE SCOTCH WHISKY
2 MEASURES BOILING WATER
1 MEASURE GINGER WINE
LEMON SLICE, TO DECORATE

Put the lemon juice and honey into a toddy glass and stir well. Add the whisky and continue stirring. Stir in the boiling water, then add the ginger wine. Decorate with a lemon slice. Stir continuously while drinking it hot.

WHISKY MAC

3–4 ICE CUBES
1 MEASURE SCOTCH WHISKY
1 MEASURE GINGER WINE

Put the ice cubes into an old-fashioned glass. Pour the whisky and ginger wine over the ice and stir slightly.

Right: Whisky Mac

BOURBON PEACH SMASH

6 MINT LEAVES
3 PEACH SLICES
3 LEMON SLICES, PLUS EXTRA TO
DECORATE
2 TEASPOONS CASTER SUGAR
2 MEASURES BOURBON WHISKEY
ICE CUBES, PLUS CRUSHED ICE,
TO SERVE
MINT SPRIG, TO DECORATE

Muddle the mint leaves, peach slices, lemon slices, and sugar in a cocktail shaker. Add the bourbon and some ice cubes and shake well. Strain into an old-fashioned glass over crushed ice. Decorate with a mint sprig and 2 lemon slices and serve with short straws.

Left: Bourbon Peach Smash

CANADIAN DAISY

4–5 ICE CUBES, PLUS EXTRA TO SERVE
2 MEASURES CANADIAN WHISKY
2 TEASPOONS LEMON JUICE
1 TEASPOON RASPBERRY JUICE
1 TEASPOON SUGAR SYRUP
SODA WATER, TO TOP UP
WHOLE RASPBERRIES, TO DECORATE
1 TEASPOON BRANDY

Put the ice cubes into a cocktail shaker with the whisky, fruit juices and sugar syrup and shake well. Strain into a tall glass. Add ice cubes and top up with soda water. Decorate with raspberries and float the brandy on top of the drink.

BLACK JACK

¾ MEASURE JACK DANIEL'S
¾ MEASURE BLACK SAMBUCA

Pour the Jack Daniel's into a shot glass. Using the back of a bar spoon, slowly float the sambuca over the Jack Daniel's.

ROLLIN' STONED

4–5 ICE CUBES, PLUS EXTRA TO SERVE
2 MEASURES THAI WHISKY
1 DASH BANANA LIQUEUR
1 DASH RASPBERRY LIQUEUR
1 DASH LIME JUICE
2 MEASURES ORANGE JUICE
2 MEASURES PINEAPPLE JUICE
ORANGES SLICES, TO DECORATE
COCKTAIL CHERRIES, TO DECORATE

Put all the ingredients into a cocktail shaker. Shake and strain into a highball glass filled with ice cubes. Decorate with orange slices and cocktail cherries, impaled on a cocktail stick. Serve with long straws.

Right: Rollin' Stoned

GODFATHER

ICE CUBES
2 MEASURES J&B RARE
SCOTCH WHISKY
1 MEASURE AMARETTO DI
SARONNO LIQUEUR

Put some ice cubes into a cocktail shaker with the whisky and Amaretto di Saronno and shake vigorously. Strain into a small old-fashioned glass filled with ice cubes.

ITALIAN HEATHER

4–5 ICE CUBES
4 MEASURES SCOTCH
WHISKY
1 MEASURE GALLIANO
LEMON RIND TWIST, TO
DECORATE

Put the ice cubes into a tall glass and stir in the whisky and Galliano. Decorate with a lemon rind twist.

LEPRECHAUN DANCER

4–5 ICE CUBES
1 MEASURE IRISH WHISKEY
1 MEASURE LEMON JUICE
SODA WATER, TO TOP UP
DRY GINGER ALE, TO TOP UP
LEMON RIND TWIST, TO DECORATE

Combine the ice cubes, whiskey and lemon juice in a highball glass. Top up with equal measures of soda water and ginger ale. Decorate with a lemon rind twist.

ROB ROY

1 ICE CUBE, CRACKED
1 MEASURE SCOTCH WHISKY
½ MEASURE VERMOUTH
1 DASH ANGOSTURA BITTERS
LEMON RIND SPIRAL, TO DECORATE

Put the cracked ice, whisky, vermouth and bitters into a mixing glass and stir well. Strain into a cocktail glass and decorate the rim with a lemon rind spiral.

Never trust any complicated cocktail that remains perfectly clear until the last ingredient goes in, and then immediately clouds.
TERRY PRATCHETT

BOBBY BURNS

4–5 CUBES
1 MEASURE SCOTCH WHISKY
1 MEASURE DRY VERMOUTH
1 TABLESPOON BÉNÉDICTINE
LEMON RIND STRIP, TO
DECORATE

Put the ice cubes into a cocktail shaker with the whisky, vermouth and Bénédictine and shake until a frost forms. Strain into a chilled cocktail glass and decorate with a lemon rind strip.

ROAMIN' THE GLOAMIN'

4–5 ICE CUBES
2 MEASURES SCOTCH
WHISKY
1 MEASURE COINTREAU
2 TABLESPOONS ORANGE
JUICE
ORANGE SLICE, TO
DECORATE

Put the ice cubes into a cocktail shaker. Add the whisky, Cointreau and orange juice and shake until a frost forms. Pour into an old-fashioned glass and decorate with an orange slice.

For art to exist, for any sort of aesthetic activity or perception to exist, a certain physiological precondition is indispensable: intoxication.
FRIEDRICH NIETZSCHE

RATTLESNAKE

4–5 ICE CUBES, PLUS EXTRA TO
SERVE
1½ MEASURES SCOTCH WHISKY
1 TEASPOON LEMON JUICE
1 TEASPOON SUGAR SYRUP
1 EGG WHITE
FEW DROPS PERNOD

Put all the ingredients into a cocktail shaker and shake very well. Strain into a glass and add more ice cubes.

Drinking is a way of ending
the day.
ERNEST HEMINGWAY

ECLIPSE

4–5 ICE CUBES, PLUS
CRUSHED ICE, TO SERVE
2 MEASURES JACK DANIEL'S
½ MEASURE CHAMBORD
½ MEASURE LIME JUICE
1 DASH SUGAR SYRUP
1 MEASURE CRANBERRY
JUICE
1 MEASURE RASPBERRY
JUICE
RASPBERRY, TO DECORATE
LIME WEDGE, TO
DECORATE

Put the ice cubes into a cocktail shaker with all the other ingredients and shake well. Strain into a large highball glass filled with crushed ice. Decorate with a raspberry and a lime wedge and serve with long straws.

BLINKER

CRACKED ICE
½ MEASURE CANADIAN WHISKY
¾ MEASURE GRAPEFRUIT JUICE
¼ MEASURE GRENADINE
ORANGE RIND TWIST, TO
DECORATE

Put some cracked ice into a cocktail shaker with the whisky, grapefruit juice and grenadine and shake well. Serve in a chilled cocktail glass and decorate with an orange rind twist.

Right: Blinker

ST CLEMENT'S MANHATTAN

ICE CUBES
1 MEASURE ORANGE-
INFUSED BOURBON
WHISKEY
1 MEASURE LEMON-
INFUSED BOURBON
WHISKEY
1 TABLESPOON SWEET
VERMOUTH
4 DASHES ANGOSTURA
BITTERS
ORANGE AND LEMON RIND
TWISTS, TO DECORATE

Put some ice cubes into a mixing glass with the whiskies, vermouth and bitters and stir well. Strain into a chilled cocktail glass and decorate with orange and lemon rind twists.

ZOOM

ICE CUBES
2 MEASURES SCOTCH
WHISKY
1 TEASPOON CLEAR HONEY
1 MEASURE CHILLED
WATER
1 MEASURE SINGLE CREAM

Put some ice cubes into a cocktail shaker, add the whisky, honey, chilled water and cream and shake well. Strain into an old-fashioned glass and serve at once.

NERIDA

4–5 ICE CUBES
JUICE OF ½ LIME OR LEMON
3 MEASURES SCOTCH WHISKY
DRY GINGER ALE, TO TOP UP
LIME OR LEMON SLICES, TO
DECORATE

Put the ice cubes, lime or lemon juice and whisky into a cocktail shaker and shake until a frost forms. Pour without straining into a chilled Collins glass. Top up with ginger ale and stir gently. Decorate with lime or lemon slices.

The problem with the world is that everyone is a few drinks behind.
HUMPHREY BOGART

GOLDEN DAISY

4–5 ICE CUBES
JUICE OF 1 LEMON
1 TEASPOON SUGAR SYRUP
½ MEASURE COINTREAU
3 MEASURES SCOTCH WHISKY
LIME WEDGE, TO DECORATE

Put the ice cubes into a cocktail shaker. Pour the lemon juice, sugar syrup, Cointreau and whisky over the ice and shake until a frost forms. Strain into an old-fashioned glass and decorate with a lime wedge.

SOUTHERLY BUSTER

4–5 ICE CUBES
1 MEASURE BLUE CURAÇAO
3 MEASURES SCOTCH WHISKY
LEMON RIND STRIP, TO DECORATE

Put the ice cubes into a mixing glass. Pour the Curaçao and whisky over the ice, stir vigorously, then strain into a chilled cocktail glass. Twist the lemon rind strip over the drink and drop it in. Serve with a straw.

SILKY PIN

ICE CUBES
1 MEASURE SCOTCH WHISKY
1 MEASURE DRAMBUIE CREAM LIQUEUR

Fill an old-fashioned glass with ice cubes and pour the whisky and Drambuie Cream Liqueur over them. Stir gently.

RUSTY NAIL

ICE CUBES
1½ MEASURES SCOTCH WHISKY
1 MEASURE DRAMBUIE

Fill an old-fashioned glass with ice cubes and pour the whisky and Drambuie over them. Stir gently.

Right: Rusty Nail

AMERICAN BELLE

½ MEASURE CHERRY LIQUEUR
½ MEASURE AMARETTO DI SARONNO LIQUEUR
½ MEASURE BOURBON WHISKEY

Pour the cherry liqueur into a shot glass. Using the back of a bar spoon, slowly float the Amaretto di Saronno over the cherry liqueur. Float the bourbon over the Amaretto in the same way.

BARBERA

5 ICE CUBES, CRACKED
1 MEASURE BOURBON WHISKEY
¾ MEASURE DRAMBUIE
¼ MEASURE AMARETTO DI SARONNO LIQUEUR
2 DASHES ORANGE BITTERS
LEMON RIND TWIST
ORANGE SLICE, TO DECORATE

Put half the cracked ice into a mixing glass with the whiskey, Drambuie, Amaretto di Saronno and bitters. Strain into a tumbler over the remaining ice cubes. Squeeze the zest from the lemon rind twist over the surface and decorate with an orange slice.

I'll admit I may have seen better days, but I'm still not to be had for the price of a cocktail, like a salted peanut.
BETTE DAVIS

CLUB

3 ICE CUBES, CRACKED
2 DASHES ANGOSTURA BITTERS
1 MEASURE SCOTCH WHISKY
1 DASH GRENADINE
LEMON RIND SPIRAL, TO DECORATE
COCKTAIL CHERRY, TO DECORATE

Put the cracked ice into a mixing glass. Add the bitters, whisky and grenadine and stir well. Strain into a cocktail glass and decorate with a lemon rind spiral and a cocktail cherry.

BOOMERANG

½ MEASURE JÄGERMEISTER
½ MEASURE BOURBON
WHISKEY

Pour the Jägermeister into a shot glass. Using the back of a bar spoon, slowly float the bourbon over the Jägermeister.

A KIWI IN TENNESSEE

½ KIWI FRUIT, PEELED
2 MEASURES JACK DANIEL'S
1 MEASURE KIWI FRUIT SCHNAPPS
1 MEASURE LEMON JUICE
ICE CUBES
LEMONADE, TO TOP UP

Muddle the kiwi fruit in a cocktail shaker, then add the Jack Daniel's, schnapps and lemon juice. Add some ice cubes and shake well. Strain into a highball glass filled with ice cubes. Stir and top up with lemonade.

Left: A Kiwi in Tennessee

LYNCHBURG LEMONADE

ICE CUBES
1½ MEASURES JACK DANIEL'S
1 MEASURE COINTREAU
1 MEASURE LEMON JUICE
LEMONADE, TO TOP UP
LEMON SLICES, TO DECORATE

Put some ice cubes into a cocktail shaker with the Jack Daniel's, Cointreau and lemon juice and shake well. Strain into a glass filled with ice cubes. Top up with lemonade and stir. Decorate with lemon slices.

ABERDEEN ANGUS

2 MEASURES SCOTCH WHISKY
1 TEASPOON CLEAR HONEY
2 TEASPOONS LIME JUICE
1 MEASURE DRAMBUIE

Combine the whisky and honey in a mug and stir until smooth. Add the lime juice. Warm the Drambuie in a small saucepan over a low heat. Pour into a ladle, ignite and pour into the mug. Stir and serve immediately.

MIKE COLLINS

5–6 ICE CUBES
JUICE OF 1 LEMON
1 TABLESPOON SUGAR SYRUP
3 MEASURES IRISH WHISKEY
ORANGE SLICE, TO DECORATE
COCKTAIL CHERRY, TO DECORATE
SODA WATER, TO TOP UP
ORANGE RIND SPIRAL, TO DECORATE

Put the ice cubes into a cocktail shaker. Pour the lemon juice, sugar syrup and whiskey over the ice and shake until a frost forms. Pour without straining into a tumbler or Collins glass and add the orange slice and cocktail cherry impaled on a cocktail stick. Top up with soda water, stir lightly and serve, decorated with an orange rind spiral.

SUBURBAN

4–5 ICE CUBES
3 DROPS ORANGE OR
ANGOSTURA BITTERS
3 MEASURES BOURBON
WHISKEY OR SCOTCH WHISKY
1 MEASURE PORT
1 MEASURE DARK RUM

Put the ice cubes into a mixing glass. Shake the bitters over the ice and pour in the bourbon or whisky, port and rum. Stir vigorously, then strain into a chilled cocktail glass.

MISSISSIPPI PUNCH

CRUSHED ICE
3 DROPS ANGOSTURA BITTERS
1 TEASPOON SUGAR SYRUP
JUICE OF 1 LEMON
1 MEASURE BRANDY
1 MEASURE DARK RUM
2 MEASURES BOURBON
WHISKEY

Half-fill a tall glass with crushed ice. Shake the bitters over the ice. Pour in the sugar syrup and the lemon juice, then stir gently to mix thoroughly. Add the brandy, rum and bourbon, in that order, stir once and serve with straws.

RITZ OLD-FASHIONED

LIGHTLY BEATEN EGG WHITE
CASTER SUGAR
3 ICE CUBES, CRUSHED
1½ MEASURES BOURBON
WHISKEY
½ MEASURE GRAND MARNIER
1 DASH LEMON JUICE
1 DASH ANGOSTURA BITTERS
ORANGE OR LEMON RIND
SPIRAL, TO DECORATE

Frost the rim of a cocktail glass by dipping it into the egg white, then pressing it into the sugar. Put the crushed ice into a cocktail shaker and add the bourbon, Grand Marnier, lemon juice and bitters. Shake to mix, then strain into the prepared glass. Decorate with and orange or lemon rind spiral.

Right: Ritz Old-Fashioned

NEW YORKER

2–3 ICE CUBES, CRACKED
1 MEASURE SCOTCH WHISKY
1 TEASPOON LIME JUICE
1 TEASPOON ICING SUGAR
FINELY GRATED RIND OF ½ LEMON
LEMON RIND SPIRAL, TO DECORATE

Put the cracked ice into a cocktail shaker and add the whisky, lime juice and sugar. Shake until a frost forms. Strain into an old-fashioned glass. Sprinkle the grated lemon rind over the surface and decorate the rim of the glass with a lemon rind spiral.

MANHATTAN

4–5 ICE CUBES
1 MEASURE SWEET VERMOUTH
3 MEASURES RYE OR BOURBON
WHISKEY
COCKTAIL CHERRY, TO
DECORATE (OPTIONAL)

Put the ice cubes into a mixing glass. Pour the vermouth and whiskey over the ice. Stir vigorously, then strain into a chilled cocktail glass. Drop in a cocktail cherry, if you like.

CASSIS

4–5 ICE CUBES
1 MEASURE BOURBON WHISKEY
1/2 MEASURE DRY VERMOUTH
1 TEASPOON CRÈME DE CASSIS
2 BLUEBERRIES, TO DECORATE

Put the ice cubes into a cocktail shaker and pour in the bourbon, vermouth and crème de cassis. Shake well, then strain into a chilled cocktail glass and decorate with blueberries impaled on a cocktail stick.

Left: Cassis

GODFATHER SOUR

ICE CUBES
1½ MEASURES BOURBON
WHISKEY
1 MEASURE AMARETTO DI
SARONNO LIQUEUR
1 MEASURE LEMON JUICE
1 TEASPOON SUGAR SYRUP
LEMON SLICES, TO
DECORATE

Put some ice cubes into a cocktail shaker with the bourbon, Amaretto di Saronno, lemon juice and sugar syrup and shake well. Strain into a small old-fashioned glass filled with ice cubes and decorate with lemon slices.

SKIPPER

4–5 ICE CUBES
4 DROPS GRENADINE
JUICE OF ½ ORANGE
1 MEASURE DRY VERMOUTH
3 MEASURES RYE WHISKEY OR
SCOTCH WHISKY
ORANGE WEDGE, TO DECORATE

Put the ice cubes into a mixing glass. Pour the grenadine over the ice and add the orange juice, vermouth and whiskey or whisky. Stir vigorously until nearly frothy, then pour into a tumbler. Decorate with an orange wedge and serve with a straw.

WHISKY SOUR

ICE CUBES
2 MEASURES SCOTCH
WHISKY
1½ MEASURES LEMON JUICE
1 EGG WHITE
2 TABLESPOONS CASTER
SUGAR
4 DASHES ANGOSTURA
BITTERS
LEMON SLICE, TO
DECORATE
COCKTAIL CHERRY, TO
DECORATE

Put some ice cubes into a cocktail shaker with the whisky, lemon juice, egg white, sugar and bitters and shake well. Strain into a sour glass filled with ice cubes and decorate with a lemon slice and a cocktail cherry.

BOURBON SLOE GIN

ICE CUBES, PLUS CRUSHED ICE,
TO SERVE
1½ MEASURES BOURBON WHISKEY
½ MEASURE SLOE GIN
½ MEASURE LEMON JUICE
1 TABLESPOON SUGAR SYRUP
LEMON AND PEACH SLICES,
TO DECORATE

Put some ice cubes into a cocktail shaker with the bourbon, sloe gin, lemon juice and sugar syrup and shake well. Strain into a cocktail glass over crushed ice. Decorate with lemon and peach slices.

HARLEQUIN

5 WHITE GRAPES, PLUS
EXTRA TO DECORATE
½ MEASURE SWEET
VERMOUTH
6 DASHES ORANGE
BITTERS
CRUSHED ICE
2 MEASURES CANADIAN
CLUB WHISKY

Muddle the grapes, vermouth and bitters in an old-fashioned glass. Half-fill the glass with crushed ice and stir well. Add the whisky and top up with crushed ice. Decorate with 2 grapes.

VANILLA DAISY

CRUSHED ICE
2 MEASURES BOURBON WHISKEY
1 MEASURE LEMON JUICE
1 MEASURE VANILLA SYRUP
1 TEASPOON GRENADINE
COCKTAIL CHERRIES, TO
DECORATE

Put some crushed ice into a cocktail shaker with the bourbon, lemon juice and vanilla syrup and shake well. Strain into an old-fashioned glass filled with crushed ice, then drizzle the grenadine through the drink. Decorate with 2 cocktail cherries impaled on a cocktail stick.

WHISKY DAISY

ICE CUBES
2 MEASURES SCOTCH WHISKY OR
BOURBON WHISKEY
1 MEASURE LEMON JUICE
1 TEASPOON CASTER SUGAR
1 TEASPOON GRENADINE
SODA WATER, TO TOP UP (OPTIONAL)
LEMON RIND SPIRAL, TO DECORATE

Put some ice cubes into a cocktail shaker with the whisky, or whiskey lemon juice, sugar and grenadine and shake well. Strain into an old-fashioned glass filled with ice cubes and top up with soda water, if you like. Decorate with a lemon rind spiral.

SICILIAN KISS

CRUSHED ICE
2 MEASURES SOUTHERN COMFORT
1 MEASURE AMARETTO DI SARONNO
LIQUEUR
LEMON SLICE, TO DECORATE

Put plenty of crushed ice into a squat glass or an old-fashioned glass with the Southern Comfort and Amaretto di Saronno and stir to mix. Garnish with a lemon slice.

WINE AND CHAMPAGNE

CHESHIRE CAT

4–5 ICE CUBES
1 MEASURE BRANDY
1 MEASURE SWEET VERMOUTH
1 MEASURE ORANGE JUICE
CHAMPAGNE, TO TOP UP
ORANGE RIND STRIP, TO DECORATE
ORANGE RIND SPIRAL, TO DECORATE

Put the ice cubes into a mixing glass. Pour the brandy, vermouth and orange juice over the ice and stir to mix. Strain into a Champagne flute and top up with Champagne. Squeeze the zest from the orange rind strip over the drink and decorate with an orange rind spiral.

CARIBBEAN CHAMPAGNE

1 TABLESPOON LIGHT RUM
1 TABLESPOON CRÈME DE BANANE
1 DASH ANGOSTURA BITTERS
CHAMPAGNE, TO TOP UP
BANANA AND PINEAPPLE SLICES, TO DECORATE
COCKTAIL CHERRY, TO DECORATE

Pour the rum, crème de banane and bitters into a chilled Champagne flute. Top up with Champagne and stir gently. Decorate with the banana and pineapple slices and cocktail cherry, all impaled on a cocktail stick.

MAN IN THE MOON

ICE CUBES
1 MEASURE VODKA
½ MEASURE APRICOT
BRANDY
½ MEASURE LEMON JUICE
2 DASHES GRENADINE
CHILLED CHAMPAGNE
OR SPARKLING WINE, TO
TOP UP

Put some ice cubes into a cocktail shaker with the vodka, apricot brandy, lemon juice and grenadine and shake well. Strain into a Champagne glass and top up with chilled Champagne or sparkling wine.

BLACK VELVET

4 MEASURES GUINNESS
4 MEASURES CHAMPAGNE

Pour the Guinness into a large glass and carefully add the Champagne.

FROBISHER

CHOPPED ICE
2 DASHES ANGOSTURA BITTERS
3 TABLESPOONS GIN
CHILLED CHAMPAGNE, TO TOP UP
LEMON RIND TWIST, TO DECORATE

Fill a highball glass with chopped ice. Shake the bitters over the ice. Pour in the gin and top up with the chilled Champagne. Squeeze the lemon rind twist over the drink and drop it in.

BELLINI

2 MEASURES PEACH JUICE
4 MEASURES CHILLED
CHAMPAGNE
1 DASH GRENADINE (OPTIONAL)
PEACH SLICE, TO DECORATE
(OPTIONAL)

Mix the peach juice and chilled Champagne in a large Champagne glass with a dash of grenadine, if using. Decorate with a peach slice, if you like.

Right: Bellini

EVE

SEVERAL DROPS PERNOD
1 TABLESPOON COGNAC
2 TEASPOONS SUGAR
2 TEASPOONS CURAÇAO
PINK CHAMPAGNE, TO TOP UP

Add the Pernod drops to a Champagne saucer; swirl gently to coat the inside of the glass. Pour in the Cognac. Soak the sugar in the Curaçao until it has dissolved, then add them to the Cognac and stir gently. Top up with pink Champagne.

ARIA CLASSIC

1 BROWN SUGAR CUBE
3 DASHES ANGOSTURA BITTERS
1 MEASURE GRAND MARNIER
CHAMPAGNE, TO TOP UP
ORANGE RIND TWIST, TO DECORATE

Drop the sugar cube into a chilled Champagne flute and shake the bitters over it. Add the Grand Marnier and stir briefly. Top up with Champagne and decorate with an orange rind twist.

CARLTON

ICE CUBES
3 MEASURES ORANGE JUICE
2 TABLESPOONS GRAND MARNIER
1 EGG WHITE
2–3 DASHES PEACH BITTERS
CHAMPAGNE, TO TOP UP
COCKTAIL CHERRIES, TO DECORATE

Put some ice cubes into a cocktail shaker and pour the orange juice, Grand Marnier, egg white and bitters over them. Shake very well. Strain into a Champagne saucer, top up with Champagne and stir gently. Decorate with cocktail cherries.

CHAMPAGNE COOLER

CRUSHED ICE
1 MEASURE BRANDY
1 MEASURE COINTREAU
CHAMPAGNE, TO TOP UP
MINT SPRIGS, TO DECORATE

Put some crushed ice into a Champagne saucer. Pour the brandy and Cointreau over the ice. Top up with Champagne and stir. Decorate with mint sprigs.

CALIFORNIA DREAMING

ICE CUBES
2 DASHES KIRSCH
3 MEASURES PINEAPPLE JUICE
1 DASH LEMON JUICE
CHILLED CHAMPAGNE, TO
TOP UP
PINEAPPLE WEDGE, TO
DECORATE

Put some ice cubes into a food processor or blender with the kirsch and fruit juices and blend for 30 seconds. Pour into a wine glass and top up with chilled Champagne. Decorate with a pineapple wedge.

LOVING CUP

8 SUGAR CUBES
2 LEMONS
½ BOTTLE MEDIUM OR
SWEET SHERRY
¼ BOTTLE BRANDY
1 BOTTLE DRY SPARKLING
WHITE WINE

Rub the sugar cubes over the lemons to absorb the zest's oils. Thinly peel the lemons and remove as much of the pith as possible. Thinly slice the lemons and set aside. Put the lemon rind, sherry, brandy and sugar cubes into a jug and stir until the sugar has dissolved. Cover and chill for about 30 minutes. To serve, add the wine to the jug and float the lemon slices on top. Serves 12.

COOL SHOWER

ICE CUBES
RIND OF 1 ORANGE
3 MEASURES SPARKLING DRY WHITE WINE
1 MEASURE CAMPARI
2 MEASURES ORANGE JUICE

Put some ice cubes into a wine goblet with the orange rind. Add the sparkling wine, Campari and orange juice.

HEAD-OVER-HEELS

4–5 ICE CUBES
JUICE OF 1 LIME
3 MEASURES VODKA
SUGAR CUBE
3 DROPS ANGOSTURA BITTERS
CHAMPAGNE, TO TOP UP

Put the ice cubes into a cocktail shaker. Pour the lime juice and vodka over the ice and shake until a frost forms. Drop a sugar cube into a glass and shake the bitters over it. Strain the contents of the cocktail shaker into the glass and top up with Champagne.

LUSH CRUSH

2 STRAWBERRIES, HULLED
1 DASH SUGAR SYRUP
2 LIME WEDGES
1 MEASURE ABSOLUT KURANT VODKA
ICE CUBES
CHAMPAGNE, TO TOP UP
STRAWBERRY SLICE, TO DECORATE

Muddle the strawberries, sugar syrup and lime wedges in a cocktail shaker. Add the vodka and some ice cubes. Shake and double strain into a chilled Champagne flute. Top up with Champagne and decorate with a strawberry slice.

CELEBRATION COCKTAIL

1 LEMON WEDGE
CASTER SUGAR
ICE CUBES
1 MEASURE BRANDY
1 DASH BÉNÉDICTINE
1 DASH CRÈME DE MURE
CHILLED CHAMPAGNE, TO TOP UP

Frost the rim of a Champagne flute by moistening it with the lemon wedge, then pressing it into the sugar. Put some ice cubes into a cocktail shaker and add the brandy, Bénédictine and crème de mure. Shake well, strain into the prepared glass and top up with Champagne.

Right: Celebration Cocktail

BUCK'S TWIZZ

1 MEASURE CHILLED ORANGE JUICE
½ MEASURE MARASCHINO LIQUEUR
1 MEASURE ABSOLUT MANDARIN VODKA
CHILLED CHAMPAGNE, TO TOP UP
RINDLESS PINK GRAPEFRUIT SLICE, TO
DECORATE

Pour the orange juice and Maraschino liqueur into a chilled Champagne saucer, then add the vodka and Champagne together (this prevents excessive fizzing). Float a rindless pink grapefruit slice on the surface.

BUCK'S FIZZ

2 MEASURES CHILLED ORANGE JUICE
6 MEASURES CHILLED CHAMPAGNE
¼ SLICES OF ORANGE, TO DECORATE

Pour the chilled orange juice into a Champagne flute or cocktail glass and add the chilled Champagne. Decorate the rim of the glass with quarter slices of orange.

Left: Buck's Fizz

KIR CHAMPAGNE ROYALE

1 TEASPOON VODKA
2 TEASPOONS CRÈME DE CASSIS
CHAMPAGNE, TO TOP UP
CHERRY, TO DECORATE

Put the vodka and crème de cassis into a Champagne saucer. Top up with Champagne and decorate with a cherry.

CAVENDISH

CHOPPED ICE
2 DROPS ANGOSTURA BITTERS
2 MEASURES VODKA
CHILLED CHAMPAGNE, TO TOP UP
LEMON RIND TWIST, TO DECORATE

Fill a highball glass with chopped ice. Shake the bitters over the ice. Pour in the vodka and top up with chilled Champagne. Squeeze the lemon rind twist over the drink and drop it in.

LIME FIZZ

1 LIME WEDGE
1 MEASURE LIME VODKA
1 MEASURE ORANGE JUICE
ICE CUBES
CHAMPAGNE, TO TOP UP
LIME RIND TWISTS, TO
DECORATE

Squeeze the lime wedge into a cocktail shaker and add the vodka and orange juice with some ice cubes. Shake very briefly and double strain into a chilled Champagne flute. Top up with Champagne and decorate with lime rind twists.

PERNOD FIZZ

1 MEASURE PERNOD
6 MEASURES CHILLED
CHAMPAGNE
LIME SLICE, TO DECORATE

Put the Pernod into a Champagne flute and swirl it round to coat the inside of the glass. Slowly pour in the chilled Champagne, allowing the drink to become cloudy. Decorate with a lime slice.

GORGEOUS GRACE

ICE CUBES
1 MEASURE BRANDY
½ MEASURE COINTREAU
CHILLED CHAMPAGNE, OR
SPARKLING DRY WHITE WINE, TO
TOP UP
ORANGE SLICE, TO DECORATE

Put some ice cubes into a mixing glass with the brandy and Cointreau and mix gently. Pour the drink into a Champagne glass and top up with chilled Champagne or sparkling wine. Decorate with an orange slice.

BUBBLE BERRY

2 RASPBERRIES
2 BLACKBERRIES, PLUS EXTRA TO
DECORATE
½ MEASURE FRAMBOISE LIQUEUR
½ MEASURE CRÈME DE MURE
3 MEASURES CHAMPAGNE

Muddle the raspberries and blackberries in a Champagne flute. Add the framboise and the crème de mure. Top up with the Champagne. Decorate the glass with a blackberry and serve with a straw immediately.

Right: Bubble Berry

BOMBAY PUNCH

ICE CUBES
1.2 LITRES (2 PINTS) BRANDY
1.2 LITRES (2 PINTS) SHERRY
150ML (¼ PINT) MARASCHINO
LIQUEUR
150ML (¼ PINT) ORANGE
CURAÇAO
5 LITRES (8 PINTS) CHILLED
CHAMPAGNE
2.5 LITRES (4 ½ PINTS) SPARKLING
MINERAL WATER
FRUIT IN SEASON, TO DECORATE
MINT SPRIGS, TO DECORATE

Put plenty of ice cubes into a large punch bowl with all the other ingredients and stir gently. Decorate with fruit and mint sprigs. Keep the punch bowl packed with ice. Serves 25–30.

Right: Bombay Punch

PADDY'S NIGHT

3 ICE CUBES, CRACKED
1 MEASURE GREEN CRÈME
DE MENTHE
1 MEASURE IRISH WHISKEY
CHAMPAGNE, TO TOP UP

Put the cracked ice into a cocktail shaker with the crème de menthe and whiskey and shake well. Strain into a Champagne flute and top up with Champagne.

CHABLIS CUP

3 RIPE PEACHES, SKINNED, STONED
AND SLICED
1 ORANGE, THINLY SLICED
COCKTAIL CHERRIES
3 TEASPOONS CASTER SUGAR
1 BOTTLE CHABLIS
4 MEASURES GRAND MARNIER
4 MEASURES KIRSCH

Put the fruit and sugar into a punch bowl. Pour in the Chablis, Grand Marnier and kirsch and stir. Cover and chill for 1 hour. Serves 15–20.

MANGO BELLINI

3 MEASURES MANGO JUICE
PINK CHAMPAGNE,
TO TOP UP

Pour the mango juice into a Champagne flute and top up with pink Champagne. Stir gently to mix and serve immediately.

LA SEINE FIZZ

1 MEASURE COGNAC
½ MEASURE FRAISE DE BOIS
½ MEASURE LEMON JUICE
1 DASH ORANGE BITTERS
2 STRAWBERRIES, HULLED
AND CHOPPED
SUGAR SYRUP, TO TASTE
3 MEASURES CHAMPAGNE
½ MEASURE GRAND
MARNIER
STRAWBERRY WEDGE, TO
DECORATE
MINT SPRIG, TO DECORATE

Put the Cognac, Fraise de Bois, lemon juice, bitters and strawberries into a cocktail shaker with sugar syrup to taste. Shake and strain into a Champagne flute. Top up with the Champagne and pour the Grand Marnier over the top. Decorate with a strawberry wedge and a mint sprig.

GRAND MIMOSA

1 MEASURE GRAND MARNIER
2 MEASURES CHILLED ORANGE JUICE
CHILLED CHAMPAGNE, TO TOP UP

Pour the Grand Marnier and chilled orange juice into a Champagne flute and top up with chilled Champagne.

GRANDADDY MIMOSA

ICE CUBES
1 MEASURE HAVANA CLUB 3-YEAR-OLD RUM
1 MEASURE ORANGE JUICE
1/2 MEASURE LEMON JUICE
CHILLED CHAMPAGNE, TO TOP UP
1 DASH GRENADINE
ORANGE RIND TWIST, TO DECORATE

Put some ice cubes into a cocktail shaker with the rum and fruit juices and shake to mix. Strain into a Champagne flute, then top up with chilled Champagne. Drop in the grenadine and decorate with an orange rind twist.

Right: Grand Mimosa (left) Grandaddy Mimosa (right)

MARTINI ROYALE

2½ MEASURES ICE-COLD
VODKA
¼ MEASURE CRÈME DE
CASSIS
CHAMPAGNE, TO TOP UP
LEMON RIND TWIST, TO
DECORATE

Pour the vodka into a chilled Martini glass, then stir in the crème de cassis. Top up with Champagne, then add a lemon rind twist.

CHAMPINO

ICE CUBES
1 MEASURE CAMPARI
1¼ MEASURES SWEET
VERMOUTH
CHILLED CHAMPAGNE, TO
TOP UP
LEMON RIND TWIST, TO
DECORATE

Put some ice cubes into a cocktail shaker with the Campari and vermouth and shake well. Strain into a chilled Martini glass. Top up with chilled Champagne and decorate with a lemon rind twist.

RITZ FIZZ I

1 DASH BLUE CURAÇAO
1 DASH LEMON JUICE
1 DASH AMARETTO DI SARONNO LIQUEUR
CHAMPAGNE, TO TOP UP
LEMON RIND SPIRAL, TO DECORATE

Pour the Curaçao, lemon juice and Amaretto di Saronno into a glass and top up with Champagne. Stir gently to mix and decorate the drink with a lemon rind spiral.

RITZ FIZZ II

ICE CUBES
½ MEASURE CRÈME DE CASSIS
½ MEASURE POIRE WILLIAM LIQUEUR
CHILLED CHAMPAGNE, TO TOP UP
PEAR SLICES, PEELED, TO DECORATE

Put some ice cubes into a mixing glass with the crème de cassis and Poire William and stir to mix well. Strain into a Champagne flute and top up with chilled Champagne. Decorate with peeled pear slices.

CHAMPAGNE JULEP

2 MINT SPRIGS, PLUS EXTRA TO
DECORATE
1 TABLESPOON SUGAR SYRUP
CRUSHED ICE
1 MEASURE BRANDY
CHAMPAGNE, TO TOP UP

Muddle the mint with the sugar syrup in a highball glass. Fill the glass with crushed ice, then add the brandy. Top up with Champagne and stir gently. Decorate with extra mint sprigs.

Left: Champagne Julep

SLINKY MINK

½ MEASURE RASPBERRY PURÉE
1 DASH SUGAR SYRUP
2 TEASPOONS LIME JUICE
CHAMPAGNE, TO TOP UP
LIME RIND TWIST, TO DECORATE

Pour the raspberry purée, sugar syrup and lime juice into the bottom of a chilled Champagne flute. Top up with Champagne, stir lightly and decorate with a lime rind twist.

Always remember that I have taken more out of alcohol then alcohol has taken out of me.
WINSTON CHURCHILL

CHAMPAGNE ROMANOV FIZZ

2 ICE CUBES
8–10 RIPE STRAWBERRIES, HULLED
4 MEASURES ORANGE JUICE
4 MEASURES CHAMPAGNE
STRAWBERRY SLICE, TO DECORATE
MINT SPRIG, TO DECORATE

Put 1 ice cube into a food processor or blender with the strawberries and orange juice and blend until smooth. Put the remaining ice cube into a tall glass and add the strawberry liquid. Top up with the Champagne. Stir briskly, decorate with a strawberry slice and a mint sprig and serve immediately.

CLASSIC CHAMPAGNE COCKTAIL

1 SUGAR CUBE
1–2 DASHES ANGOSTURA BITTERS
1 MEASURE BRANDY
CHILLED CHAMPAGNE, TO TOP UP
ORANGE SLICE, TO DECORATE

Saturate the sugar cube with the bitters, then drop it into a chilled cocktail glass or Champagne flute. Add the brandy, then top up with chilled Champagne. Decorate with an orange slice.

There can't be good living where there is not good drinking.
BENJAMIN FRANKLIN

RUSSIAN SPRING PUNCH

ICE CUBES
½ MEASURE CRÈME DE CASSIS
1 MEASURE LEMON JUICE
2 TABLESPOONS SUGAR SYRUP
CHILLED CHAMPAGNE, TO TOP UP
2 MEASURES ABSOLUT VODKA
LEMON SLICE, TO DECORATE
BERRIES, TO DECORATE

Fill a sling glass with ice cubes. Pour over the crème de cassis, lemon juice and sugar syrup. Add the chilled Champagne and vodka at the same time (this prevents excessive fizzing) and stir. Decorate with a lemon slice and berries.

PARISIAN SPRING PUNCH

ICE CUBES, PLUS CRUSHED ICE, TO SERVE
1½ MEASURES CALVADOS
½ MEASURE LEMON JUICE
½ MEASURE NOILLY PRAT VERMOUTH
1 TEASPOON CASTER SUGAR
CHILLED CHAMPAGNE, TO TOP UP
APPLE SLICES, TO DECORATE

Put some ice cubes into a cocktail shaker with the Calvados, lemon juice, vermouth and sugar and shake to mix. Strain into a sling glass over crushed ice and top up with chilled Champagne. Decorate with apple slices.

THE CLASSIC'S CLASSIC

1 SUGAR CUBE
2 DASHES ANGOSTURA
BITTERS
1 MEASURE GRAND MARNIER
4 MEASURES CHILLED
CHAMPAGNE
ORANGE RIND, TO DECORATE

Saturate the sugar cube with the bitters, then drop it into a Champagne flute. Add the Grand Marnier, then top up with the chilled Champagne. Drop the orange rind into the drink to decorate.

Right: The Classic's Classic

TEQUILA

MEXICANA

8–10 ICE CUBES
1¼ MEASURES TEQUILA
¾ MEASURE FRAMBOISE
LIQUEUR
¾ MEASURE LEMON JUICE
3½ MEASURES PINEAPPLE JUICE
PINEAPPLE WEDGE, TO
DECORATE
LEMON SLICE, TO DECORATE

Put half the ice cubes into a cocktail shaker with the tequila, framboise and fruit juices and shake vigorously for about 10 seconds. Pour the drink into a large highball glass over the remaining ice cubes and decorate with a pineapple wedge and a lemon slice.

MARACUJA

1 FRESH RIPE PASSION FRUIT
4–5 ICE CUBES
1¼ MEASURES GOLD TEQUILA
1 TABLESPOON CRÉOLE SHRUBB
¾ MEASURE LIME JUICE
2 TEASPOONS COINTREAU
1 TEASPOON PASSION FRUIT SYRUP
PHYSALIS (CAPE GOOSEBERRY),
TO DECORATE

Cut the passion fruit in half and scoop the flesh into a cocktail shaker. Add the ice cubes, tequila, Créole Shrubb, lime juice, Cointreau and passion fruit syrup and shake vigorously for 10 seconds. Strain through a fine sieve into a chilled cocktail glass. Decorate with a physalis.

Right: Maracuja

FOREST FRUIT

1 LIME WEDGE
SOFT BROWN SUGAR
2 BLACKBERRIES, PLUS EXTRA
TO DECORATE
2 RASPBERRIES, PLUS EXTRA
TO DECORATE
2 TEASPOONS CHAMBORD
2 TEASPOONS CRÈME DE
MURE
1¼ MEASURES TEQUILA
2 TEASPOONS COINTREAU
1¼ MEASURES LEMON JUICE
CRUSHED ICE
LEMON SLICES, TO
DECORATE

Frost the rim of an old-fashioned glass by moistening it with the lime wedge, then pressing it into the sugar. Drop the blackberries and raspberries into the glass and muddle to a pulp. Stir in the Chambord and crème de mure. Pour in the tequila, Cointreau and lemon juice, fill with crushed ice and stir gently, lifting the muddled berries from the bottom of the glass. Decorate with lemon slices, a blackberry and a raspberry.

BORDER CROSSING

ICE CUBES
1½ MEASURES GOLD TEQUILA
1 MEASURE LIME JUICE
1 MEASURE CLEAR HONEY
4 DASHES ORANGE BITTERS
3 MEASURES DRY GINGER ALE
BLUEBERRIES, TO DECORATE
LIME WEDGES, TO DECORATE

Put some ice cubes into a cocktail shaker with the tequila, lime juice, honey and bitters and shake well. Pour into a highball glass and top up with the ginger ale. Decorate with blueberries and lime wedges.

BAJA SOUR

4–5 ICE CUBES
1¼ MEASURES GOLD TEQUILA
2 TEASPOONS SUGAR SYRUP
1¼ MEASURES LEMON JUICE
2 DASHES ORANGE BITTERS
½ EGG WHITE
1 TABLESPOON AMONTILLADO SHERRY
LEMON SLICES, TO DECORATE
ORANGE RIND SPIRAL, TO DECORATE

Put the ice cubes into a cocktail shaker with the tequila, sugar syrup, lemon juice, bitters and egg white and shake vigorously. Pour into a large sour glass and drizzle the sherry over the drink. Decorate with lemon slices and an orange rind spiral.

COBALT MARGARITA

1 LIME WEDGE
FINE SEA SALT
4–5 ICE CUBES
1¼ MEASURES TEQUILA
2 TEASPOONS COINTREAU
½ MEASURE BLUE CURAÇAO
¾ MEASURE LIME JUICE
¾ MEASURE GRAPEFRUIT JUICE
LIME RIND SPIRAL, TO DECORATE

Frost the rim of a chilled cocktail glass by moistening it with a lime wedge, then pressing it into salt. Put the ice cubes into a cocktail shaker with the tequila, Cointreau, Curaçao and fruit juices and shake vigorously for 10 seconds. Strain into the prepared glass. Decorate with a lime rind spiral.

SUNBURN

ICE CUBES
¾ MEASURE GOLD TEQUILA
1 TABLESPOON COINTREAU
6 MEASURES CRANBERRY JUICE
ORANGE SLICE, TO DECORATE

Fill a large highball glass with ice cubes and pour in the tequila, Cointreau and cranberry juice. Decorate with an orange slice.

SOMBRERO

4–5 ICE CUBES
¾ MEASURE GOLD TEQUILA
¾ MEASURE WHITE CRÈME DE CACAO
3½ MEASURES SINGLE CREAM
GRATED NUTMEG, TO DECORATE

Put the ice cubes into a cocktail shaker. Pour in the tequila, crème de cacao and cream and shake vigorously for 10 seconds. Strain into a chilled Margarita glass. Sprinkle with grated nutmeg and serve with a straw.

TEQUILA DE COCO

CRUSHED ICE
1 MEASURE TEQUILA
1 MEASURE LEMON JUICE
1 MEASURE COCONUT SYRUP
3 DASHES MARASCHINO LIQUEUR
LEMON SLICE, TO DECORATE

Put some crushed ice into a food processor or blender and add the tequila, lemon juice, coconut syrup and Maraschino liqueur. Blend for a few seconds, then pour into a Collins glass and decorate with a lemon slice.

TEQUINI

ICE CUBES
3 DASHES ORANGE BITTERS
3 MEASURES TEQUILA
BLANCO
2 TEASPOONS DRY FRENCH
VERMOUTH, PREFERABLY
NOILLY PRAT
BLACK OLIVE, TO DECORATE

Fill a mixing glass with ice cubes, then add the bitters and tequila. Stir gently for 10 seconds. Put the vermouth into a chilled cocktail glass and swirl to coat the inside, then tip it out. Stir the bitters and tequila for a further 10 seconds and strain into the cocktail glass. Decorate with a black olive.

MEXICAN MULE

1 LIME
1 DASH SUGAR SYRUP
CRUSHED ICE
1 MEASURE JOSÉ CUERVO GOLD
TEQUILA
1 MEASURE KAHLÚA
DRY GINGER ALE, TO TOP UP

Cut the lime into slices, put them into a highball glass and muddle with the sugar syrup. Half-fill the glass with crushed ice and add the tequila and Kahlúa. Stir well, then top up with ginger ale.

PINK CADILLAC CONVERTIBLE

3 LIME WEDGES
FINE SEA SALT
ICE CUBES
1¼ MEASURES GOLD
TEQUILA
½ MEASURE CRANBERRY
JUICE
¾ MEASURE GRAND
MARNIER
LIME WEDGE, TO DECORATE

Frost the rim of a large old-fashioned glass by moistening it with a lime wedge, then pressing it into the salt. Fill the glass with ice cubes. Pour the tequila and cranberry juice into a cocktail shaker. Squeeze the juice from the remaining lime wedges into the shaker, pressing the rind to release its oils, then drop the wedges in. Add 4–5 ice cubes and shake vigorously for 10 seconds, then strain into the prepared glass. Drizzle the Grand Marnier over the top and decorate with lime a wedge.

THIGH HIGH

3 STRAWBERRIES, HULLED
1 TEASPOON STRAWBERRY SYRUP
4–5 ICE CUBES
1 MEASURE TEQUILA
1 MEASURE DARK CRÈME DE CACAO
1½ MEASURES SINGLE CREAM
1 STRAWBERRY DIPPED IN COCOA
POWDER, TO DECORATE

Muddle the strawberries and strawberry syrup in a cocktail shaker. Add the ice cubes with the tequila, crème de cacao and cream and shake to mix. Strain into a large, chilled cocktail glass and decorate with a strawberry dipped in cocoa powder.

BROOKLYN BOMBER

5 ICE CUBES, CRUSHED
1 MEASURE TEQUILA
½ MEASURE COINTREAU
½ MEASURE CHERRY BRANDY
½ MEASURE GALLIANO
1 MEASURE LEMON JUICE
ORANGE SLICE, TO DECORATE
COCKTAIL CHERRY, TO
DECORATE

Put half the crushed ice into a cocktail shaker and add the tequila, Cointreau, cherry brandy, Galliano and lemon juice. Shake to mix and pour it into a hurricane glass over the remaining ice. Decorate with an orange slice and a cocktail cherry and serve with straws.

The first drink with water, the second
without water, the third like water.
SPANISH MAXIM

JALISCO SWIZZLE

4–5 ICE CUBES, PLUS CRUSHED ICE,
TO SERVE
3 DASHES ANGOSTURA BITTERS
¾ MEASURE GOLD TEQUILA
¾ MEASURE GOLDEN RUM
1¼ MEASURES LIME JUICE
¾ MEASURE PASSION FRUIT JUICE
2 TEASPOONS SUGAR SYRUP
SODA WATER, TO TOP UP
LIME SLICE, TO DECORATE
MINT SPRIG, TO DECORATE

Put the ice cubes into a cocktail shaker with the bitters, tequila, rum, fruit juices and sugar syrup and shake vigorously. Strain into a highball glass filled with crushed ice. Top up with soda water and stir briefly until a frost forms. Decorate with a lime slice and a mint sprig.

SOUR APPLE

4–5 ICE CUBES
1¼ MEASURES TEQUILA
2 TEASPOONS COINTREAU
1 TABLESPOON APPLE SCHNAPPS
¾ MEASURE LIME JUICE
¾ MEASURE UNSWEETENED APPLE
JUICE
GRANNY SMITH APPLE WEDGE, TO
DECORATE

Put the ice cubes into a cocktail shaker with the tequila, Cointreau, schnapps and fruit juices and shake vigorously for 10 seconds. Strain into a chilled cocktail glass. Decorate with an apple wedge.

Right: Sour Apple

VIVA MARIA

ICE CUBES, PLUS CRUSHED ICE, TO SERVE
1 MEASURE TEQUILA
½ MEASURE LIME JUICE
¼ MEASURE MARASCHINO LIQUEUR
½ TEASPOON GRENADINE
½ EGG WHITE
LEMON AND LIME SLICES, TO DECORATE
COCKTAIL CHERRY, TO DECORATE

Put some ice cubes into a cocktail shaker and pour the tequila, lime juice, Maraschino liqueur, grenadine and egg white over them. Shake well and strain into a Champagne saucer filled with crushed ice. Decorate with lemon and lime slices and a cocktail cherry.

MARGARITA

1 LIME WEDGE
ROCK SALT
ICE CUBES
2 MEASURES HERRADURA REPOSADO TEQUILA
1 MEASURE LIME JUICE
1 MEASURE TRIPLE SEC
LIME SLICE, TO DECORATE

Frost the rim of a Margarita glass by moistening it with a lime wedge, then pressing it into the salt. Put some ice cubes into a cocktail shaker with the tequila, lime juice and Triple Sec. Shake well. Strain into the prepared glass. Decorate with a lime slice.

Right: Margarita

MEXICOLA

4 LIME WEDGES
CRUSHED ICE
1¼ MEASURES TEQUILA
6 MEASURES COLA

Muddle the lime wedges in a large highball glass. Fill the glass with crushed ice, then pour in the tequila and cola. Stir gently, lifting the lime wedges through the drink.

RUBY RITA

1¼ MEASURES PINK GRAPEFRUIT
JUICE
FINE SEA SALT
ICE CUBES
1¼ MEASURES GOLD TEQUILA
¾ MEASURE COINTREAU
PINK GRAPEFRUIT WEDGE, TO
DECORATE

Frost the rim of an old-fashioned glass by moistening it with some of the pink grapefruit juice, then pressing it into the salt. Fill the glass with ice cubes. Pour the tequila, Cointreau and the remaining pink grapefruit juice into a cocktail shaker, fill it with ice cubes and shake vigorously. Strain into the prepared glass and decorate with a pink grapefruit wedge. Serve with straws.

Right: Ruby Rita

DIRTY SANCHEZ

ICE CUBES
2 TEASPOONS NOILLY PRAT VERMOUTH
2 MEASURES GOLD TEQUILA (PREFERABLY AÑEJO)
2 TEASPOONS BRINE FROM A JAR OF BLACK OLIVES
BLACK OLIVES, TO DECORATE

Fill a mixing glass with ice cubes and add the vermouth. Stir to coat the ice, then discard the excess vermouth. Add the tequila and brine and stir until thoroughly chilled. Strain into a chilled cocktail glass and decorate with 2 black olives impaled on a cocktail stick.

FROSTBITE

4–5 ICE CUBES
1 MEASURE TEQUILA
1 MEASURE DOUBLE CREAM
1 MEASURE WHITE CRÈME DE CACAO
½ MEASURE WHITE CRÈME DE MENTHE
DRINKING CHOCOLATE POWDER, TO DECORATE

Put the ice cubes into a cocktail shaker. Pour in the tequila, cream, crème de cacao and crème de menthe and shake vigorously for 10 seconds. Strain into a chilled cocktail glass. Sprinkle with drinking chocolate powder.

TEXAS TEA

ICE CUBES
¾ MEASURE TEQUILA
1 TABLESPOON WHITE RUM
1 TABLESPOON COINTREAU
2 TEASPOONS SUGAR SYRUP
¾ MEASURE LEMON JUICE
¾ MEASURE ORANGE JUICE
3½ MEASURES STRONG
FRUIT TEA, CHILLED
ORANGE AND LEMON
SLICES, TO DECORATE
MINT SPRIG, TO DECORATE

Put a handful of ice cubes into a cocktail shaker with the tequila, rum, Cointreau, sugar syrup, fruit juices and tea and shake vigorously. Strain into a sling glass filled with ice cubes. Decorate with orange and lemon slices and a mint sprig.

GRAND MARGARITA

1 LIME WEDGE, PLUS EXTRA
TO DECORATE
ROCK SALT
ICE CUBES
1½ MEASURES SILVER
TEQUILA
1 MEASURE GRAND
MARNIER
1 MEASURE LIME JUICE

Frost the rim of a Margarita glass by moistening it with the lime wedge, then pressing it into the salt. Put some ice cubes into a cocktail shaker with the tequila, Grand Marnier and lime juice and shake well. Double strain into the prepared glass and decorate with a lime wedge.

RUDE COSMOPOLITAN

ICE CUBES
1½ MEASURES GOLD
TEQUILA
1 MEASURE COINTREAU
1 MEASURE CRANBERRY
JUICE
½ MEASURE LIME JUICE
LIME WEDGE DUSTED
IN COCOA POWDER, TO
DECORATE

Put some ice cubes into a cocktail shaker, add the tequila, Cointreau and fruit juices and shake well. Strain into a chilled Martini glass and decorate with a lime wedge dusted in cocoa powder.

SOUTH OF THE BORDER

4–5 ICE CUBES
1¼ MEASURES TEQUILA
¾ MEASURE KAHLÚA
1¼ MEASURES LIME JUICE

Put the ice cubes into a cocktail shaker with the tequila, Kahlúa and lime juice and shake vigorously for 10 seconds. Strain the drink into a chilled cocktail glass.

DESERT DAISY

CRUSHED ICE
1 MEASURE TEQUILA
1¼ MEASURES LIME JUICE
2 TEASPOONS SUGAR SYRUP
1 TABLESPOON FRAISE DE BOIS
BLACKBERRY AND STRAWBERRY, TO
DECORATE
LIME AND ORANGE WEDGES, TO
DECORATE
MINT SPRIG, TO DECORATE

Half-fill a large old-fashioned glass with crushed ice. Pour in the tequila, lime juice and sugar syrup and stir gently until a frost forms. Add more crushed ice, then float the Fraise de Bois on top. Decorate with a blackberry, a strawberry, a lime wedge, an orange wedge and a mint sprig.

PLAYA DEL MAR

1 ORANGE SLICE
LIGHT BROWN SUGAR AND
SEA SALT, MIXED
ICE CUBES
1¼ MEASURES GOLD TEQUILA
¾ MEASURE GRAND MARNIER
2 TEASPOONS LIME JUICE
¾ MEASURE CRANBERRY JUICE
¾ MEASURE PINEAPPLE JUICE
PINEAPPLE WEDGE, TO
DECORATE
ORANGE RIND SPIRAL, TO
DECORATE

Frost the rim of a sling glass by moistening it with the orange slice, then pressing it into the sugar and salt mixture. Fill the glass with ice cubes. Pour the tequila, Grand Marnier and fruit juices into a cocktail shaker. Fill the shaker with ice cubes and shake vigorously for 10 seconds, then strain into the prepared glass. Decorate with a pineapple wedge and an orange rind spiral.

SILK STOCKING

DRINKING CHOCOLATE
POWDER
4–5 ICE CUBES
¾ MEASURE TEQUILA
¾ MEASURE WHITE CRÈME
DE CACAO
3½ MEASURES SINGLE
CREAM
2 TEASPOONS GRENADINE

Frost the rim of a chilled cocktail glass by dipping it into water, then pressing it into the drinking chocolate powder. Put the ice cubes into a cocktail shaker with the tequila, crème de cacao, cream and grenadine. Shake vigorously for 10 seconds, then strain the drink into the prepared glass.

PALE ORIGINAL

ICE CUBES
2 MEASURES GOLD
TEQUILA
½ MEASURE GINGER
SYRUP
½ MEASURE LIME JUICE
1 MEASURE GUAVA JUICE
LIME WEDGES, TO
DECORATE

Put some ice cubes into a cocktail shaker with the tequila, ginger syrup and fruit juices and shake well. Strain into a chilled cocktail glass. Decorate with a lime wedge.

RASPBERRY BERET

½ MEASURE LIGHT CRÈME
DE CACAO
1 MEASURE CHILLED GOLD
TEQUILA
1 PLUMP RASPBERRY

Pour the crème de cacao into a shot glass. Using the back of a bar spoon, slowly float the tequila over the crème de cacao. Slowly lower the raspberry into the drink – it will settle between the 2 spirits.

EL DIABLO

ICE CUBES
1¼ MEASURES TEQUILA GOLD
¾ MEASURE LIME JUICE
2 TEASPOONS GRENADINE
3½ MEASURES DRY GINGER ALE
LIME SLICE, TO DECORATE

Fill a large highball glass with ice cubes and pour in the tequila, lime juice and grenadine. Top up with ginger ale and stir gently. Decorate with a lime slice.

BECKONING LADY

6–8 ICE CUBES
2 MEASURES TEQUILA
4 MEASURES PASSION FRUIT JUICE
1–2 TEASPOONS GALLIANO
COCKTAIL CHERRIES, TO
DECORATE

Fill a hurricane or highball glass with the ice cubes. Using the back of a bar spoon, slowly add the tequila and passion fruit juice and stir well to mix. Float the Galliano on top in a layer about 1 cm (half an inch) deep and decorate with cocktail cherries.

BATANGA

1 MEXICAN LIME
ROCK SALT
ICE CUBES
2 MEASURES TEQUILEÑO
BLANCO TEQUILA
MEXICAN COLA, TO TOP UP

Cut the tip off the lime and make a slit in its side. Dip in the salt and run it around the rim of an old-fashioned glass. Fill the glass with ice cubes and add the tequila. Squeeze half of the lime juice into the drink, then stir it with the knife used to cut the lime while topping up the drink with Mexican cola.

Right: Batanga

TIJUANA SLING

ICE CUBES
1¼ MEASURES TEQUILA
¾ MEASURE CRÈME DE CASSIS
¾ MEASURE LIME JUICE
2 DASHES PEYCHAUD'S BITTERS
3½ MEASURES DRY GINGER ALE
LIME SLICE, TO DECORATE
BLACKCURRANTS OR BLUEBERRIES, TO DECORATE

Put some ice cubes into a cocktail shaker with the tequila, crème de cassis, lime juice and bitters and shake vigorously. Pour into a large sling glass, then top up with ginger ale. Decorate with a lime slice and some blackcurrants or blueberries impaled on a cocktail stick.

CADILLAC

3 LIME WEDGES
FINE SEA SALT
1¼ MEASURES GOLD TEQUILA
½ MEASURE COINTREAU
1¼ MEASURES LIME JUICE
4–5 ICE CUBES
2 TEASPOONS GRAND MARNIER
LIME SLICE, TO DECORATE

Frost the rim of a chilled cocktail glass by moistening it with a lime wedge, then pressing it into the salt. Pour the tequila, Cointreau and lime juice into a cocktail shaker. Squeeze the juice from the remaining lime wedges into the shaker, pressing the rind to release its oils, and drop the wedges in. Add the ice cubes and shake vigorously for 10 seconds, then strain into the prepared glass. Drizzle the Grand Marnier over the top and decorate with a lime slice.

MEXICAN BULLDOG

ICE CUBES
¾ MEASURE TEQUILA
¾ MEASURE KAHLÚA
1¼ MEASURES SINGLE
CREAM
3½ MEASURES COLA
DRINKING CHOCOLATE
POWDER, TO DECORATE

Put some ice cubes into a highball glass. Pour in the tequila, Kahlúa and cream, then top up with the cola. Stir gently and serve decorated with drinking chocolate powder.

PANCHO VILLA

4–5 ICE CUBES
1 MEASURE TEQUILA
½ MEASURE TIA MARIA
1 TEASPOON COINTREAU

Put the ice cubes into a cocktail shaker and pour in the tequila, Tia Maria and Cointreau. Shake until a frost forms, then strain into a chilled cocktail glass.

BRAVE BULL

ICE CUBES
¾ MEASURE TEQUILA
¾ MEASURE KAHLÚA

Fill an old-fashioned glass with ice cubes. Pour in the tequila and Kahlúa and stir gently.

PASSION FRUIT MARGARITA

LIME WEDGE
COARSE SEA SALT
ICE CUBES
1½ MEASURES GOLD TEQUILA
1 MEASURE COINTREAU
1 TEASPOON PASSION FRUIT SYRUP
1 MEASURE FRESH LIME JUICE
PULP AND SEEDS OF 1 PASSION
FRUIT
MINT SPRIG, TO DECORATE

Frost the rim of a Margarita glass by moistening it with a lime wedge, then pressing it into the salt. Put some ice cubes into a cocktail shaker with the tequila, Cointreau, passion fruit syrup, lime juice and half of the passion fruit pulp and shake well. Double strain into the prepared glass. Add the remaining passion fruit pulp and decorate with a mint sprig.

Right: Passion Fruit Margarita

ACAPULCO BLISS

4–5 ICE CUBES
¾ MEASURE TEQUILA
1 TABLESPOON PISANG AMBON
(BANANA LIQUEUR)
2 TEASPOONS GALLIANO
¾ MEASURE LEMON JUICE
3½ MEASURES PASSION FRUIT JUICE
¾ MEASURE SINGLE CREAM
LEMON SLICES, TO DECORATE
PINEAPPLE WEDGE, TO DECORATE
MINT SPRIG, TO DECORATE

Put the ice cubes into a cocktail shaker with the tequila, Pisang Ambon, Galliano, fruit juices and cream and shake vigorously. Pour into a large sling glass and decorate with lemon slices, a pineapple wedge and a mint sprig.

> Sometimes too much to drink is barely enough.
> **MARK TWAIN**

TEQUILA SLAMMER

1 MEASURE GOLD TEQUILA
1 MEASURE CHAMPAGNE

Pour the tequila into a shot glass. Slowly top it up with Champagne. Cover the top of the glass with the palm of your hand to seal the contents inside and grip it with your fingers. Briskly pick up the glass and slam it down on to a surface to make the drink fizz, then quickly gulp it down in one, while it is still fizzing.

ALLELUIA

ICE CUBES
¾ MEASURE TEQUILA
½ MEASURE BLUE CURAÇAO
2 TEASPOONS MARASCHINO SYRUP
1 DASH EGG WHITE
¾ MEASURE LEMON JUICE
3½ MEASURES BITTER LEMON
LEMON SLICE, TO DECORATE
COCKTAIL CHERRY, TO DECORATE
MINT SPRIG, TO DECORATE

Put 4–5 ice cubes into a cocktail shaker with the tequila, Curaçao, Maraschino syrup, egg white and lemon juice and shake vigorously. Strain into a large highball glass filled with ice cubes. Top up with the bitter lemon and stir gently. Decorate with a lemon slice, a cocktail cherry and a mint sprig.

HONEY WATER

4–5 ICE CUBES
1¼ MEASURES GOLD
TEQUILA
¾ MEASURE SWEET
VERMOUTH
3 DASHES ANGOSTURA
BITTERS
3 DASHES PEYCHAUD'S
BITTERS
2 TEASPOONS GRAND
MARNIER
COCKTAIL CHERRY, TO
DECORATE
ORANGE RIND SPIRAL, TO
DECORATE

Put the ice cubes into a mixing glass, pour in the tequila, vermouth and bitters and stir gently for 10 seconds. Put the Grand Marnier into a chilled cocktail glass, swirl it round to coat the inside of the glass, then tip it out. Stir the contents of the mixing glass again for 10 seconds then strain into the cocktail glass. Decorate with a cocktail cherry impaled on a cocktail stick and an orange rind spiral.

AGAVE JULEP

8 MINT LEAVES, TORN
1 TABLESPOON SUGAR SYRUP
1¼ MEASURES GOLD TEQUILA
1¼ MEASURES LIME JUICE
CRUSHED ICE
LIME WEDGE, TO DECORATE
MINT SPRIG, TO DECORATE

Muddle the mint leaves with the sugar syrup in a highball glass. Add the tequila and lime juice, fill the glass with crushed ice and stir vigorously to mix. Decorate with a lime wedge and a mint sprig.

Right: Agave Julep

ROSARITA BAY BREEZE

ICE CUBES
1¼ MEASURES TEQUILA
6 MEASURES CRANBERRY JUICE
1½ MEASURES PINEAPPLE JUICE
ORANGE SLICE, TO DECORATE

Put some ice cubes into a large highball glass and pour in the tequila and cranberry juice. Float the pineapple juice on top and decorate with an orange slice.

TEQUILA SUNRISE

ICE CUBES
2 MEASURES TEQUILA
4 MEASURES ORANGE JUICE
2 TEASPOONS GRENADINE
ORANGE SLICES, TO DECORATE
COCKTAIL CHERRY, TO
DECORATE

Left: Tequila Sunrise

Put some ice cubes into a cocktail shaker with the tequila and orange juice and shake to mix. Strain into a highball glass filled with ice cubes. Slowly pour in the grenadine and allow it to settle. Decorate with an orange slice and a cocktail cherry.

SOUTH FOR THE SUMMER

2 TEASPOONS GRENADINE
CRUSHED ICE
2 MEASURES TEQUILA
3 MEASURES ORANGE JUICE
4 PINEAPPLE CHUNKS
PINEAPPLE LEAF, TO DECORATE
ORANGE RIND, TO DECORATE

Spoon the grenadine into a highball glass. Put some crushed ice into a food processor or blender with the tequila, orange juice and pineapple chunks and blend until slushy. Pour the mixture over the grenadine, decorate with a pineapple leaf and an orange twist and stir just before serving.

ROOSTER BOOSTER

ICE CUBES
1¼ MEASURES TEQUILA
6 MEASURES GRAPEFRUIT
JUICE
1 TABLESPOON GRENADINE
3½ MEASURES SODA WATER
LIME SLICE, TO DECORATE
COCKTAIL CHERRY, TO
DECORATE

Put some ice cubes into a large highball glass. Pour in the tequila, grapefruit juice and grenadine, stir gently, then top up with soda water. Decorate with a lime slice and a cocktail cherry.

MOCKINGBIRD

ICE CUBES
1¼ MEASURES TEQUILA
¾ MEASURE GREEN CRÈME DE
MENTHE
1¼ MEASURES LIME JUICE
LEMON RIND SPIRAL, TO DECORATE

Put some ice cubes into a cocktail shaker with the tequila, crème de menthe and lime juice and shake vigorously for about 10 seconds. Strain into a chilled cocktail glass. Decorate with a lemon rind spiral.

Right: Mockingbird

OTHER SPIRITS AND LIQUEURS

SLIPPERY NIPPLE

1 MEASURE SAMBUCA
½ MEASURE BAILEYS IRISH
CREAM

Pour the sambuca into a shot glass. Using the back of a bar spoon, slowly float the Baileys over the sambuca.

GO WEST

ICE CUBES
½ MEASURE FRANGELICO
HAZELNUT LIQUEUR
1 MEASURE LIMONCELLO
1 MEASURE DRY WHITE WINE
½ MEASURE SUGAR SYRUP
½ MEASURE LEMON JUICE
LEMON RIND TWIST, TO DECORATE

Put some ice cubes into a cocktail shaker with the Frangelico, limoncello, wine, sugar syrup and lemon juice and shake well. Double strain into a chilled Martini glass. Decorate with a lemon rind twist.

Right: Go West

STRAWBERRY ECLAIR

1 STRAWBERRY, HULLED
1 LIME WEDGE
½ MEASURE FRANGELICO
HAZELNUT LIQUEUR
½ MEASURE WILD
STRAWBERRY LIQUEUR
ICE CUBES

Muddle the strawberry and the lime wedge in a cocktail shaker. Add the liqueurs and some ice cubes, then shake briefly and strain into a shot glass.

B-4-12

½ MEASURE AMARETTO DI
SARONNO LIQUEUR
½ MEASURE BAILEYS IRISH
CREAM
½ MEASURE CHILLED
ABSOLUT KURANT VODKA

Pour the Amaretto di Saronno into a shot glass. Using the back of a bar spoon, slowly float the Baileys over the Amaretto. Pour the Absolut Kurant over the Baileys in the same way.

MONEY SHOT

1 MEASURE WELL-CHILLED
JÄGERMEISTER
1 MEASURE WELL-CHILLED RUMPLE
MINZE (PEPPERMINT LIQUEUR)

Pour the Jägermeister into a shot glass. Using the back of a bar spoon, slowly float the Rumple Minze over the Jägermeister.

QF

½ MEASURE KAHLÚA
DASH MIDORI
½ MEASURE BAILEYS IRISH
CREAM

Pour the Kahlúa into a shot glass. Using the back of a bar spoon, slowly float the Midori over the Kahlúa. Float the Baileys over the Midori in the same way.

SAKE-TINI

ICE CUBES
2½ MEASURES SAKE
1 MEASURE VODKA
½ MEASURE ORANGE CURAÇAO
CUCUMBER WHEELS, TO DECORATE

Put some ice cubes into a mixing glass, add the sake, vodka and Curaçao and stir well. Strain into a chilled cocktail glass and add 2 cucumber wheels, which are made by peeling the cucumber in strips lengthwise and then thinly slicing.

ABSINTHE MINDED

ICE CUBES
1 MEASURE ABSINTHE
1 DASH LEMON JUICE
1 DASH CHAMBORD

Put some ice cubes into a cocktail shaker with all the other ingredients and shake briefly. Strain into a chilled shot glass.

Left: Absinthe Minded

BATIDA

CRUSHED ICE
2 MEASURES CACHAÇA
½ MEASURE SUGAR SYRUP
½ MEASURE LEMON JUICE
3 MEASURES FRUIT JUICE
(STRAWBERRY, PINEAPPLE OR
MANGO)

Fill a highball glass with crushed ice. Pour the cachaça, sugar syrup and fruit juices into the glass and stir to mix thoroughly.

COWGIRL

1 MEASURE CHILLED PEACH
SCHNAPPS
½ MEASURE BAILEYS IRISH CREAM
PEACH WEDGE, TO DECORATE

Pour the chilled schnapps into a shot glass. Using the back of a bar spoon, slowly layer the Baileys over the schnapps. Place a peach wedge on the rim of the glass, to be eaten after the shot has been drunk.

PANSY

ICE CUBES
½ MEASURE PERNOD
SEVERAL DASHES GRENADINE
FEW DASHES ANGOSTURA BITTERS
LEMON RIND TWIST, TO DECORATE

Put some ice cubes into a cocktail shaker and pour the Pernod, grenadine and bitters over them. Shake well. Pour into a chilled cocktail glass and decorate with a lemon rind twist.

CUCUMBER SAKE-TINI

ICE CUBES
2½ MEASURES CUCUMBER-INFUSED SAKE
1½ MEASURES GIN
½ MEASURE ORANGE CURAÇAO
PEELED CUCUMBER SLICES, TO DECORATE

Put some ice cubes into a mixing glass with all the other ingredients and stir until thoroughly chilled. Strain into a chilled Martini glass. Decorate with peeled cucumber slices.

GRAPPA STREGA

ICE CUBES
1 MEASURE GRAPPA (ITALIAN GRAPE BRANDY)
1 MEASURE STREGA HERBAL LIQUEUR
1 TABLESPOON LEMON JUICE
1 TABLESPOON ORANGE JUICE

Put some ice cubes into a mixing glass. Pour the grappa, Strega and fruit juices over the ice and stir. Strain into a chilled Martini glass.

GRAPPA MANHATTAN

ICE CUBES
2 MEASURES GRAPPA (ITALIAN GRAPE BRANDY)
1 MEASURE MARTINI ROSSO
½ MEASURE MARASCHINO LIQUEUR
2 DASHES ANGOSTURA BITTERS
OLIVES, TO DECORATE

Put some ice cubes into a mixing glass. Pour the grappa, Martini, Maraschino liqueur and bitters over the ice and stir. Strain into a chilled Martini glass and decorate with olives impaled on a cocktail stick.

Right: Grappa Manhattan

KIWI CAIPIROSKA

½ KIWI FRUIT, PEELED
½ LIME, CUT INTO WEDGES
2 TEASPOONS SUGAR SYRUP
CRUSHED ICE
2 MEASURES VODKA
2 TEASPOONS KIWI FRUIT
SCHNAPPS
KIWI FRUIT SLICE, TO DECORATE

Muddle the kiwi fruit, lime and sugar syrup in an old-fashioned glass. Fill the glass with crushed ice, then add the vodka and stir. Add more crushed ice, then drizzle the schnapps over the surface and decorate with a kiwi fruit slice.

ORIGINAL PISCO SOUR

ICE CUBES
2 MEASURES PISCO (SOUTH
AMERICAN GRAPE BRANDY)
1 MEASURE LEMON JUICE
2 TEASPOONS CASTER
SUGAR
1 EGG WHITE
3 DASHES ANGOSTURA
BITTERS
LEMON WEDGES, TO
DECORATE (OPTIONAL)

Put some ice cubes into a cocktail shaker with the pisco, lemon juice, sugar and egg white and shake well. Strain into an old-fashioned glass. Add the bitters to the drink's frothy head and decorate with lemon wedges, if you like.

PAPA G

ICE CUBES
1 MEASURE AMARETTO DI
SARONNO LIQUEUR
1 DASH LEMON JUICE
1 DASH SUGAR SYRUP
1 DROP ANGOSTURA BITTERS

Put some ice cubes into a cocktail shaker with all the other ingredients and shake briefly. Strain into a shot glass.

Happiness is… finding two olives in your martini when you're hungry.

JOHNNY CARSON

BANSHEE

ICE CUBES
1 MEASURE WHITE CRÈME DE CACAO
1 MEASURE CRÈME DE BANANE
1 MEASURE SINGLE CREAM

Put some ice cubes into a cocktail shaker. Pour the crème de cacao, crème de banane and cream over the ice. Shake vigorously. Strain and serve straight up.

PCP

ICE CUBES
¾ MEASURE XANTE PEAR LIQUEUR
1 DASH STRAWBERRY LIQUEUR
1 DASH PEAR LIQUEUR
1 DASH LEMON JUICE
1 DASH VANILLA SYRUP

Put some ice cubes into a cocktail shaker with all the other ingredients and shake briefly. Strain into a chilled shot glass.

Right: PCP

VELVET HAMMER

ICE CUBES
1 MEASURE COINTREAU
1 MEASURE TIA MARIA
1 MEASURE CREAM

Fill a cocktail shaker three-quarters full with ice cubes. Add all the other ingredients and shake well. Strain into a chilled cocktail glass.

CAIPIRINHA

1 LIME, QUARTERED
2 TEASPOONS CANE SUGAR
CRUSHED ICE
2 MEASURES CACHAÇA

Muddle the lime quarters and sugar in an old-fashioned glass. Fill it with crushed ice and pour the cachaça over it. Stir and add more ice if needed.

Right: Caipirinha

ATACAMA PISCO SOUR

CRUSHED ICE
1½ MEASURES PISCO (SOUTH AMERICAN
GRAPE BRANDY)
½ MEASURE BLENDED SCOTCH WHISKY
1 MEASURE LEMON JUICE
1 MEASURE SUGAR SYRUP
GRATED LEMON RIND, TO DECORATE

Put a small scoop of crushed ice into a food processor or blender with the pisco, whisky, lemon juice and sugar syrup and blend until smooth. Pour into a Margarita glass and decorate with grated lemon rind.

383

1 TEASPOON FRANGELICO HAZELNUT
LIQUEUR
1 MEASURE CHILLED STOLICHNAYA
RAZBERI VODKA
ORANGE WEDGE DUSTED WITH SUGAR, TO
DECORATE
POWDER, TO DECORATE

Put the Frangelico into a shot glass, then add the vodka. Decorate with the sugared orange wedge. Drink the shot in one gulp, then eat the orange wedge.

STRAWBERRY AND HAZELNUT LASSI

CRUSHED ICE
3 STRAWBERRIES, HULLED
⅓ BANANA
1 MEASURE FRANGELICO HAZELNUT LIQUEUR
1 MEASURE BAILEYS IRISH CREAM
2 MEASURES NATURAL YOGURT
3 MINT LEAVES, PLUS EXTRA SPRIG TO DECORATE

Put a scoop of crushed ice into a food processor or blender with all the other ingredients and blend until smooth. Pour into a tall sling glass and decorate with a mint sprig.

FIREBALL

½ MEASURE ICE-COLD KÜMMEL
½ MEASURE GOLDSCHLÄGER
½ MEASURE ABSINTHE

Pour the kümmel into a shot glass. Using the back of a bar spoon, slowly float the Goldschläger over the kümmel. Pour the absinthe over the Goldschläger in the same way.

ON THE LAWN

ICE CUBES
1 MEASURE PIMM'S NO. 1
1 MEASURE GIN
2 MEASURES LEMONADE
2 MEASURES DRY GINGER ALE
CUCUMBER STRIPS, TO DECORATE
BLUEBERRIES, TO DECORATE
ORANGE SLICES, TO DECORATE

Fill a highball glass with ice cubes, then add the Pimm's, gin, lemonade and ginger ale. Decorate with cucumber strips, blueberries and orange slices.

CLASSIC PIMM'S

2 MEASURES PIMM'S NO. 1
6–8 ICE CUBES
ORANGE, LEMON AND CUCUMBER SLICES
4 MEASURES LEMONADE
MINT OR BORAGE SPRIGS, TO DECORATE

Pour the Pimm's into a highball glass, add the ice cubes and the fruit and cucumber slices, then pour in the lemonade. Decorate with mint or borage sprigs.

Left: Classic Pimm's

MOTH AND MOOSE

½ MEASURE PASSOA
PASSION FRUIT LIQUEUR
½ MEASURE GREY GOOSE
L'ORANGE VODKA

Pour the Passoa into a shot glass. Using the back of a bar spoon, slowly float the vodka over the Passoa.

GRASSHOPPER

1 MEASURE CRÈME DE
CACAO
1 MEASURE CRÈME DE
MENTHE
⅓ MEASURE SINGLE CREAM
MINT SPRIG, TO DECORATE

Pour the crème de cacao into a cocktail glass. Using the back of a bar spoon, float the crème de menthe over the crème de cacao. Then float the cream over the crème de menthe in the same way. Decorate with a mint sprig.

BATIDA MARACUJA

ICE CUBES, PLUS CRUSHED
ICE, TO SERVE
2 MEASURES CACHAÇA
PULP OF 2 PASSION FRUIT
1 MEASURE SUGAR SYRUP
1 MEASURE LEMON JUICE
LEMON SLICES, TO
DECORATE

Put some ice cubes into a cocktail shaker with the cachaça, passion fruit pulp, sugar syrup and lemon juice and shake. Strain into a highball glass filled with crushed ice. Decorate with lemon slices and serve with straws.

BRAIN HAEMORRHAGE

1 MEASURE PEACH SCHNAPPS
1 DASH BAILEYS IRISH CREAM
3 DROPS GRENADINE

Pour the schnapps into a chilled shot glass. Using the back of a bar spoon, slowly float the Baileys over the schnapps. Very gently, drop the grenadine on top of the Baileys – it will gradually ease through this top layer.

Meet me down in the bar!
We'll drink breakfast together.

T FROTHINGILL BELLOWS,
THE BIG BROADCAST OF 1938

BUBBLE GUM

ICE CUBES
½ MEASURE PISANG
AMBON (BANANA LIQUEUR)
½ MEASURE MALIBU
1 DASH FRAISE LIQUEUR
1 DASH PINEAPPLE JUICE

Put some ice cubes into a cocktail shaker with all the other ingredients and shake briefly. Strain into a shot glass.

Dost thou think, because thou art virtuous, there shall be no more cakes and ale?
WILLIAM SHAKESPEARE, TWELFTH NIGHT

FLAMING LAMBORGHINI

1 MEASURE KAHLÚA
1 MEASURE SAMBUCA
1 MEASURE BAILEYS IRISH CREAM
1 MEASURE BLUE CURAÇAO

Pour the Kahlúa into a warmed cocktail glass. Gently pour half the sambuca over the back of a bar spoon into the cocktail glass, so that it floats on top. Pour the Baileys and the Curaçao into 2 shot glasses. Next, pour the remaining sambuca into a warmed wine glass and carefully set it alight. Pour it into the cocktail glass with care. Pour the Baileys and Curaçao into the lighted cocktail glass at the same time. Serve with a straw.

B-52

½ MEASURE KAHLÚA
½ MEASURE BAILEYS IRISH CREAM
½ MEASURE GRAND MARNIER

Pour the Kahlúa into a shot glass. Using the back of a bar spoon, slowly float the Baileys over the Kahlúa. Float the Grand Marnier over the Baileys in the same way.

VIRGIN COCKTAILS

BITTER SWEET

CRUSHED ICE
150 ML (¼ PINT) SPARKLING MINERAL
WATER
2 DASHES ANGOSTURA BITTERS
6–8 MINT LEAVES
LEMON OR LIME SLICES, TO DECORATE

Put some crushed ice into a cocktail shaker, pour 2 tablespoons of the mineral water and the bitters over it and add the mint leaves. Shake until a frost forms. Pour into a chilled glass, top up with the remaining mineral water and decorate with lemon or lime slices.

VIRGIN COLADA

CRUSHED ICE
1 MEASURE COCONUT
CREAM
2 MEASURES PINEAPPLE
JUICE
PINEAPPLE WEDGE, TO
DECORATE

Put some crushed ice into a food processor or blender with the coconut cream and pineapple juice and blend, or shake in a cocktail shaker. Pour into a tall glass and decorate with a pineapple wedge. Serve with a tall straw.

FROSTY LIME

1 SCOOP LIME SORBET
1 MEASURE GRAPEFRUIT JUICE
4 TEASPOONS MINT SYRUP
MINT STRIPS, TO DECORATE
LEMON SLICES, TO DECORATE

Put the sorbet, grapefruit juice and mint syrup into a food processor or blender and blend at high speed for about 30 seconds. Strain into a Champagne glass and decorate with mint strips and lemon slices.

CRANBERRY CRUSH

CRUSHED ICE
1.8 LITRES (3 PINTS) CRANBERRY JUICE
600 ML (1 PINT) ORANGE JUICE
600 ML (1 PINT) DRY GINGER ALE
ORANGE AND LEMON WEDGES, TO DECORATE

Half-fill a large punch bowl with crushed ice. Pour in the fruit juices and stir to mix. Top up with the ginger ale and decorate with orange and lemon wedges. Serves 15.

KEEP SOBER

ICE CUBES
½ MEASURE GRENADINE
½ MEASURE LEMON SYRUP
3 MEASURES TONIC WATER
SODA WATER, TO TOP UP

Put some ice cubes into a tumbler with the grenadine, lemon syrup and tonic water and stir together. Top up with soda water.

COOL PASSION

500 ML (17 FL OZ) ORANGE
AND PASSION FRUIT JUICE
1 LITRE (1¾ PINTS)
PINEAPPLE JUICE
1.5 LITRES (2½ PINTS)
LEMONADE
CRUSHED ICE
BLACKBERRIES, TO
DECORATE
MINT SPRIGS, TO
DECORATE

Pour the fruit juices into a large jug. Stir well to mix. Just before serving, stir in the lemonade. Pour into glasses filled with crushed ice and decorate each with a blackberry and a mint sprig. Serves 20.

PEACH, PEAR AND RASPBERRY CRUSH

CRUSHED ICE
1 RIPE PEACH, SKINNED, STONED AND CHOPPED
1 RIPE PEAR, PEELED, CORED AND CHOPPED
125 G (4 OZ) RASPBERRIES
7 MEASURES PEACH JUICE
PEAR SLICES, TO DECORATE

Put some crushed ice into a food processor or blender with the peach, pear, raspberries and peach juice and blend until smooth. Serve in cocktail glasses and decorate with pear slices. Serves 2–3.

WARBINE COOLER

2 DASHES ANGOSTURA
BITTERS
1 DASH LIME JUICE
GINGER BEER, TO TOP UP
LIME SLICES, TO DECORATE

Stir the bitters and lime juice together in a large wine glass. Top up with ginger beer and decorate with lime slices. Serve with a straw.

LIMEADE

6 LIMES
125 G (4 OZ) CASTER SUGAR
750 ML (1¼ PINTS) BOILING
WATER
PINCH OF SALT
ICE CUBES
LIME WEDGES, TO DECORATE
MINT LEAVES, TO DECORATE

Halve the limes, then squeeze the juice into a large jug. Put the squeezed lime halves into a heatproof jug with the sugar and boiling water and leave to infuse for 15 minutes. Add the salt, stir the infusion well, then strain it into the jug with the lime juice. Add 6 ice cubes, cover and chill for 2 hours or until chilled. To serve, put 3–4 ice cubes in each glass and pour the limeade over them. Decorate each glass with a lime wedge and a mint leaf. Serves 8.

Right: Limeade

MIDSUMMER PUNCH

125G (4 OZ) SUGAR
300 ML (½ PINT) WATER
300 ML (½ PINT) ORANGE JUICE
300 ML (½ PINT) PINEAPPLE JUICE
600 ML (1 PINT) COLD WEAK TEA,
STRAINED
ORANGE, LEMON, APPLE AND
PINEAPPLE SLICES
CRUSHED ICE
300 ML (½ PINT) DRY GINGER ALE
MINT SPRIGS, TO DECORATE

Put the sugar and water into a saucepan and stir over a low heat until the sugar has dissolved. Leave to cool, then pour into a large jug or bowl. Stir in the fruit juices and cold tea, then add the fruit slices and some crushed ice. To serve, pour into tall glasses and top up with the dry ginger ale. Decorate with mint sprigs. Serves 8–10.

HONEYMOON

CRUSHED ICE
1 MEASURE CLEAR HONEY
OR MAPLE SYRUP
4 TEASPOONS LIME JUICE
1 MEASURE ORANGE JUICE
1 MEASURE APPLE JUICE
COCKTAIL CHERRY, TO
DECORATE

Put some crushed ice into a cocktail shaker and add the honey or maple syrup and the fruit juices. Shake well, then strain into a chilled cocktail glass. Decorate with a cocktail cherry impaled on a cocktail stick.

TROPICAL TREAT

900 ML (1½ PINTS) YOGHURT
1 LARGE PINEAPPLE, PEELED AND ROUGHLY
CHOPPED
300 ML (½ PINT) SPARKLING MINERAL WATER
ICE CUBES
SUGAR SYRUP, TO TASTE
MINT SPRIGS, TO DECORATE

Put the yogurt, pineapple and mineral water into a food processor and blend until smooth, in batches if necessary. Put ice cubes into a tall jug, then pour the drink in through a very fine sieve. Stir, then add sugar syrup to taste and stir again. Pour into tall glasses and decorate with mint sprigs. Serves 4.

GRAPEFRUIT COOLER

125 G (4 OZ) SUGAR
4 MEASURES WATER
HANDFUL OF MINT SPRIGS,
PLUS EXTRA TO DECORATE
JUICE OF 4 LARGE LEMONS
450 ML (¾ PINT) GRAPEFRUIT
JUICE
CRUSHED ICE
SODA WATER, TO TOP UP

Put the sugar and water into a heavy-based saucepan and stir over a low heat until the sugar has dissolved. Leave to cool. Crush the mint leaves and stir into the syrup. Cover and leave to stand for about 12 hours, then strain into a jug. Add the fruit juices to the strained syrup and stir well. Fill 6 old-fashioned glasses or tumblers with crushed ice and pour the cooler into the glasses. Top up with soda water and decorate with mint sprigs. Serves 6.

ALCOHOL-FREE SANGRIA

1 LITRE (1¾ PINTS) ORANGE JUICE
SUGAR SYRUP, TO TASTE
2 LITRES (3½ PINTS) RED GRAPE JUICE
JUICE OF 6 LEMONS
JUICE OF 6 LIMES
20–30 ICE CUBES
ORANGE, LEMON AND LIME SLICES, TO
DECORATE

Pour the orange juice and sugar syrup, to taste, into a punch bowl and stir. Add the fruit juices and stir well to mix. Add the ice cubes, then float the fruit slices on top. Serves 20.

TENDERBERRY

CRUSHED ICE
6–8 STRAWBERRIES,
HULLED
1 MEASURE GRENADINE
1 MEASURE DOUBLE
CREAM
1 MEASURE DRY GINGER
ALE
GROUND GINGER, FOR
SPRINKLING
STRAWBERRY, TO
DECORATE

Put some crushed ice into a blender or food processor with the strawberries, grenadine and cream and blend for 30 seconds. Pour into a glass. Add the ginger ale and stir. Sprinkle a little ground ginger on top and decorate with a strawberry.

ANITA

3 ICE CUBES
1 MEASURE ORANGE JUICE
1 MEASURE LEMON JUICE
3 DASHES ANGOSTURA
BITTERS
SODA WATER, TO TOP UP
LEMON AND ORANGE
SLICES, TO DECORATE

Put the ice cubes into a cocktail shaker. Pour in the fruit juices and bitters and shake well. Strain into a tumbler and top up with soda water. Decorate with lemon and orange slices.

PINK TONIC

4–6 ICE CUBES
2–3 DASHES ANGOSTURA
BITTERS
8 MEASURES TONIC WATER
LIME WEDGE, TO
DECORATE

Put the ice cubes into a tumbler. Shake the bitters over the ice, add the tonic water and stir well. Decorate with a lime wedge.

RIVER CRUISE

500 G (1 LB) CANTALOUPE MELON PULP
GRATED RIND AND JUICE OF 2 LEMONS
2 TABLESPOONS SUGAR
600 ML (1 PINT) CHILLED SODA WATER

Remove and discard any melon seeds. Put the pulp into a blender or food processor and blend until smooth. Scrape the melon purée into a large jug. Put the lemon rind and juice into a small saucepan with the sugar and stir over a low heat until the sugar has dissolved. Strain the lemon mixture into the melon purée, mix well and chill. Stir in the chilled soda water just before serving. Serves 4–6.

PROHIBITION PUNCH

4 MEASURES SUGAR SYRUP
350 ML (12 FL OZ) LEMON JUICE
900 ML (1½ PINTS) APPLE JUICE
ICE CUBES
2.5 LITRES (4 PINTS) DRY GINGER ALE
ORANGE SLICES, TO DECORATE

Put the sugar syrup and fruit juices into a large chilled jug and stir. Add the ice cubes and pour in the ginger ale. Decorate with orange slices. Serves 25–30.

CARROT CREAM

5 ICE CUBES
2 MEASURES CARROT JUICE
3 MEASURES SINGLE CREAM
1 EGG YOLK
1 MEASURE ORANGE JUICE
ORANGE SLICES, TO
DECORATE

Put the ice cubes into a tall glass. Put the carrot juice, cream, egg yolk and orange juice into a cocktail shaker and shake well. Pour the carrot drink over the ice cubes. Decorate with orange slices and serve immediately.

GRENADINE SODA

½ SCOOP ORANGE SORBET
½ SCOOP RASPBERRY SORBET
1½ TABLESPOONS GRENADINE
JUICE OF ½ LIME
1 SCOOP VANILLA ICE CREAM
4 MEASURES SODA WATER
FINELY CHOPPED ORANGE SLICE, TO
DECORATE
RASPBERRIES, TO DECORATE

Put the sorbets, grenadine and lime juice into a food processor or blender and blend until slushy. Pour into a glass and put the vanilla ice cream on top. Top up with soda water. Stir gently and decorate with the finely chopped orange slice and raspberries. Serve with straws.

JERSEY LILY

ICE CUBES
5 MEASURES SPARKLING APPLE JUICE
2 DASHES ANGOSTURA BITTERS
¼ TEASPOON CASTER SUGAR
COCKTAIL CHERRY, TO DECORATE

Put some ice cubes into a cocktail shaker with the apple juice, bitters and sugar. Shake well, then strain into a wine glass. Decorate with a cocktail cherry.

SAN FRANCISCO

3 ICE CUBES
1 MEASURE ORANGE JUICE
1 MEASURE LEMON JUICE
1 MEASURE PINEAPPLE JUICE
1 MEASURE GRAPEFRUIT
JUICE
2 DASHES GRENADINE
1 EGG WHITE
SODA WATER, TO TOP UP
LEMON AND LIME SLICES, TO
DECORATE
COCKTAIL CHERRY, TO
DECORATE
ORANGE RIND SPIRAL, TO
DECORATE

Put the ice cubes into a cocktail shaker and pour in the fruit juices, grenadine and egg white. Shake well, then strain into a large goblet. Top up with soda water and decorate with lemon and lime slices, a cocktail cherry impaled on a cocktail stick and an orange rind spiral. Serve with straws.

DR LAWRENCE BRADFORD:

What is a cocktail dress?

PAULA BRADFORD:

Something to spill cocktails on.

THE EX-MRS. BRADFORD

FLORENTINE COFFEE

HOT ESPRESSO COFFEE
1 DROP ALMOND ESSENCE
1 SUGAR CUBE (OPTIONAL)

Pour the coffee into a warmed cup or heatproof glass. Add the almond essence and sugar, if using, and stir.

ROMANOV FIZZ

4–5 RIPE STRAWBERRIES, HULLED
2 MEASURES ORANGE JUICE
1 ICE CUBE
2 MEASURES SODA WATER

Put the strawberries and orange juice into a food processor or blender and blend until smooth. Put the ice cube into a sour or wine glass and add the strawberry liquid. Pour the soda water into the food processor or blender, blend briefly and use to top up the glass. Stir briskly and serve.

CLAYTON'S PUSSYFOOT

3 ICE CUBES, CRACKED
½ MEASURE LEMON SYRUP
½ MEASURE ORANGE
JUICE
1 MEASURE COLA

Put all the ingredients into a cocktail shaker and shake well. Strain into a cocktail glass.

SPICED GINGER PUNCH

2 ORANGES
CLOVES, TO TASTE
1 CM (½ INCH) PIECE OF
FRESH ROOT GINGER,
PEELED AND GRATED
2 LITRES (3½ PINTS) DRY
GINGER ALE
CINNAMON STICK

Stud the oranges with the cloves, then bake them in a preheated oven at 180°C (350°F), Gas Mark 4 for about 25 minutes, until they are a rich, golden colour. Cut the oranges into slices using a sharp knife, then put them into a saucepan with the ginger, ginger ale and the cinnamon stick. Bring steadily just to the boiling point, but do not boil. Remove the cinnamon stick, then pour the punch into heatproof glasses and serve. Serves 12.

NURSERY FIZZ

CRUSHED ICE
3 MEASURES ORANGE JUICE
3 MEASURES DRY GINGER
ALE
COCKTAIL CHERRY, TO
DECORATE
ORANGE SLICE, TO
DECORATE

Fill a large wine glass with crushed ice and pour in the orange juice and ginger ale. Decorate with a cocktail cherry and an orange slice impaled on a cocktail stick.

COCO-OCO

CRUSHED ICE
4 TEASPOONS CREAMED COCONUT OR
COCONUT SYRUP
2 TEASPOONS LEMON JUICE
1 TEASPOON MARASCHINO SYRUP
3½ MEASURES FULL-FAT MILK
4 DASHES ANGOSTURA BITTERS
PINEAPPLE LEAF AND WEDGE, TO DECORATE
COCKTAIL CHERRY, TO DECORATE

Put some crushed ice into a blender or food processor and add the creamed coconut or coconut syrup, lemon juice, Maraschino syrup, milk and bitters. Blend for a few seconds. Pour into a tall glass and decorate with a pineapple leaf and wedge and a cocktail cherry.

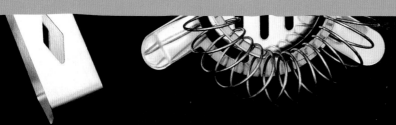

BAR BASICS

EQUIPMENT

Some pieces of equipment, such as shakers and decent glasses, are vital for any cocktail party, while others, like ice buckets, can be obtained at a later date if needed. Below is a wishlist for anyone who wants to make cocktails regularly.

Shakers
The most obvious piece of equipment is a cocktail shaker. There are two basic types, European and Boston. The basic difference between the two is that the European shaker has an integral strainer, while the Boston shaker does not. One half of the Boston shaker may be made of glass and have measurements etched into it. When mixing different cocktails, it is vital that the shaker and other equipment be cleaned thoroughly and dried between cocktails. Imagine what a trace of coconut milk from a Piña Colada would do to the taste of a Vodka Martini…

Strainers
If you are using a Boston shaker, you will need something to strain the cocktails through. Although a small sieve would work, a proper cocktail strainer looks far more stylish. Some drinks require double-straining for extra smoothness.

Measures
Getting the balance of flavours right is important for all cocktails, so the different ingredients need to be measured accurately. A set of measures makes this much easier. It is also far easier to make layered drinks by pouring the liqueurs from a measure than when trying to hold a heavy bottle steady.

Utensils
As so many drinks contain, or are decorated with, fruit, a good, sharp knife and a chopping board are essential. You will also need spoons for stirring and muddling drinks, and for floating one liqueur over another in layered drinks. A long-handled bar spoon is perfect for this. Try to get one with a spiral handle as this will make creating citrus-rind spirals much easier. Although these can be made with a small, sharp knife, a fruit parer makes this job easier. Tongs or a small scoop for ice are useful and an ice bucket may be helpful. A machine for crushing ice might be a boon if you are making cocktails regularly, but otherwise a clean tea towel, a plastic bag and a wooden rolling pin will suffice. A good corkscrew is a must and while a fork can be used to whisk egg whites, using a small whisk is quicker.

Equipment for decorating
Many drinks are decorated with fruit impaled on cocktail sticks and these are available in wood, plastic or glass. Exotic drinks may be prettified with a paper umbrella and several long drinks are served with straws or swizzle sticks.

Glasses

In order to serve cocktails, it is important to have good-quality glasses that are appropriate to the drinks. Cheap glasses will spoil both the look and the taste of your drinks, so making your efforts a waste of time.

Nowadays, cocktails are divided into several groups, loosely characterized by the type of glass in which they are served.

Classic cocktails, such as Manhattans, are, naturally enough, served in long-stemmed cocktail glasses. They are mostly either stirred or shaken with ice – in the case of the Martini, whether to shake or stir has been a subject of debate for years – and then strained into a glass. Margaritas are served in their own glasses, while Daiquiris can be served in either type.

Long drinks, such as Gin Fizz and Cuba Libre, are generally served in highball glasses, although you could also buy sling, hurricane and Collins glasses. Long drinks are usually a combination of spirits and a mixer such as fruit juice or soda water. Most are served over ice. They are often decorated with fruit.

Short drinks, such as Mai Tai, Negroni and Screwdriver, usually consist of a mixture of two spirits or one spirit and a small amount of mixer. They are served in heavy-bottomed, old-fashioned glasses – also known as rocks or lowball glasses – although some can be served in cocktail glasses. Like long drinks, these are meant for sipping slowly, and many are served with copious amounts of crushed ice. Sour glasses can probably wait until later.

Champagne cocktails, such as Bellini, Buck's Fizz and Black Velvet, and those made with other sparkling wines are served in tall Champagne flutes or wide Champagne saucers. Punches are served from a large bowl into individual glasses.

Shots are extra-short drinks, designed to be drunk in one go. Some, like the Tequila Slammer, consist of a single spirit, although others, like Slippery Nipple, are layered.

INGREDIENTS

It would be impossible to stock the ingredients necessary for every conceivable cocktail, so it is best to think about what you are planning to do. If you are going to serve a few select cocktails, you can limit what you buy, but if you are planning to do it in style, you will need a larger selection. The best idea in this case is to buy the ingredients for several of the most popular cocktails and gradually add to them. However, if you know one of your guests has a favourite cocktail, make sure you have the ingredients needed. You can also suit the drinks to the occasion: people will probably want different drinks before an alfresco summer lunch than they do at an evening cocktail party in winter.

Liquid ingredients
Start off with those commonly used in cocktails: gin, whisky, rum, vodka, brandy and tequila, as well as sparkling wines and Champagne. Added to this, you will want to have all the basic mixers, such as soda water, tonic water, cola, lemonade and fruit juices, as well as commonly used flavourings and syrups. Dry and sweet vermouth occur in quite a few gin- and vodka-based cocktails, so are good staples.

For shots, it may be best to concentrate on the ingredients for a few popular ones – there is little point in buying expensive ingredients that will just sit on a shelf untouched.

Other ingredients
Make sure you have other ingredients that you might need such as cream, cocoa power, coconut milk, salt, pepper, Tabasco sauce, Worcestershire sauce and eggs.

Ice
Ice is an integral part of making all but a few cocktails, so you need plenty of this. If you have an ice-maker in your refrigerator, make sure you empty it regularly over the preceding few days so you have a good stock of ice. Otherwise, buy a couple of bags of ice cubes the day before and put them in the freezer. When drinks are served with ice, always put as much ice in as the recipe calls for. Although you might think that more ice would dilute the drink, in fact it has the opposite effect. With more ice in, the drink stays chilled for longer so the ice does not melt.

Flavourings and decorations
Lemons, limes and oranges are musts, as are olives and cocktail cherries. Other fruit that it is good to have to hand are apples, pineapple and bananas. Mint appears as a decoration or flavouring in so many cocktails that it is a good idea to have a packet in the refrigerator. Try to use the fruits mentioned for decorations, although these can be substituted when a particular fruit is not in season. However, if a particular fruit is an integral part of the drink, it is best not to experiment.

TECHNIQUES

Although watching an experienced barman juggling a cocktail shaker round the bar can be enjoyable, it is not actually necessary to do this in order to mix a cocktail well, although that does not mean you cannot have fun practising. many cocktails.

Chilling

Always make sure that the glasses and cocktail shaker are cold. Glasses can be put into the freezer for an hour or so before use. If washing up the shaker between mixing drinks, run it under cold water before drying it off. Serve drinks as soon as possible after they are finished, in order to prevent them warming up.

Mixing drinks

There are two methods of doing this, shaking and stirring. The first incorporates the various liquids used in a drink thoroughly and chills them. It is important to shake the ingredients really thoroughly to mix them and cool them down. When flavourings such as berries are used, shaking extracts their flavours. Drinks are stirred in the glass when the ingredients combine easily. Always stir gently, to avoid incorporating air or breaking the ice cubes.

Muddling

Muddling is used in such drinks as Mint Julep. It means to crush the ingredients in the bottom of a glass to extract their flavour before the alcohol is added.

Layering

This technique, used in shots and such drinks as Irish Coffee, takes time to master. Pour the first ingredient into the glass and then add the second by pouring it gently over the back of a bar spoon held just above the first ingredient. It is important to add the liqueurs in the order specified in the recipe, that is, heaviest liqueur first, otherwise a heavier liquid will simply sink through a lighter one below and spoil the effect.

Decorating with fruit

Fruit wedges are a popular addition to many cocktails and are simple to make. They can be perched on the side of the glass, or dropped or squeezed in. Citrus wedges can be prepared in advance if you wish, but apples, pineapple and bananas are best done at the last moment. Small clusters of berries, such as redcurrants, can be draped over the rim of a glass, while cocktail cherries, berries such as raspberries and blackberries and wedges of larger fruit can be impaled on cocktail sticks and balanced on the rim or dropped into a short glass. Citrus rind can be formed into twists or spirals to dangle over the edge of a glass. Spirals are cut with a fruit parer or small, sharp knife, while twists are wider and so better cut with a vegetable peeler. For a twist, wrap the cut length round the handle of a bar spoon, or a straw or swizzle stick. Hold it for a few minutes and as its essential oils evaporate, it will dry into a spiral. Try squeezing the juice from a citrus twist onto the top of the drink for extra zing. To flame a citrus twist, hold a piece of rind with no pith attached skin-side down about 10 cm (4 in) above the drink in one hand with a lighted long match in the other. Pinch the rind firmly so that the oils spray into the flame and ignite onto the drink.

Frosting

This technique, best known in the Margarita, is worth mastering. The rim of the glass is dipped into a shallow dish of beaten egg white, water or citrus juice and then rolled in, for example, salt, sugar or cocoa powder.

INDEX

INDEX

123RF a41cats 19 above, 157, 158-159, 170; alex_1 245; alexsalcedo1 139; Andreas Argirakis 69 above, 110, 113; Angel Luis Simon Martin 182; Antonio Balaguer Soler 96-97; Beata Aldridge 328-329; belchonock 6 centre, 92; Bogdan Bratu 191; Boris Ryzhkov 223, 348; Brent Hofacker 2, 6 below, 8-9, 16, 54, 76, 91, 99, 101, 123, 135, 165, 225, 257, 272, 286, 292-293, 324, 354-355, 361; Charles Wollertz 74, 116, 178, 193, 212, 227, 241, 253, 353; Christian Jung 345; Comaniciu Dan 148; Dmitry Lobanov 151; fedorkondratenko 379; fesenko 228; foodandmore 64-65, 372-373; Gabe Palmer 79, 177; Gennadiy Poznyakov 121; gresei 34; Heinz Leitner 105; Ivan Danik 7 above, 363; Jodie Johnson 188; Maksim Shebeko 181, 307; Marcin Lukaszewicz 7 centre 133; Mikhail Valeev 7 below, 144; Nadezhda Prokudina 298; nikkiphoto 260-261; Olaf Speier 201; Oleksandr Prokopenko 210, 265, 291; Petr Goskov 6 above, 319; Piotr Krześlak 161; srapulsar38 16; starkovphoto 194; Tab1962 56; Unal Ozmen 115; Volodymyr Krasyuk 231; wawri 220-221; wiktory 176; yelo34 48; ziashusha 248. **Dreamstime.com** Grafvision 23. **Getty Images** Instants 18.

Octopus Publishing Group Jean Cazals 262, 369; Neil Mersh 59, 80, 106, 107, 229, 243; Sandra Lane 268; Stephen Conroy 13, 20, 26, 29, 31, 33, 36, 39, 42, 44, 45, 47, 49, 50, 60, 62 above, 62 below, 63, 78, 94, 95, 109, 111, 119, 124, 129, 136, 140, 141, 147, 154, 160, 162, 163 above, 163 below, 168, 169, 172, 175, 179, 187, 196, 199, 203, 205, 207, 208, 211, 214 below, 216 above, 216 below, 219, 232, 235, 239, 247, 266, 271, 275, 283, 284 above, 284 below, 304, 309 below, 312 below, 313, 315, 320, 331, 332, 333, 334, 337, 339, 340, 341, 343, 347 above, 347 below, 351; William Reavell 11, 15, 19 below, 21, 30, 52, 66, 67, 68, 69 below, 71, 72, 73, 77, 82, 83, 84, 87, 89, 100, 118, 131, 152, 153, 184, 197, 214 above, 254, 263, 267, 269, 274, 277, 279, 280, 281 above, 281 below, 288, 295, 296, 297, 299, 300, 303, 309 above, 310, 311, 312 above, 316, 317 above, 317 below, 321, 323, 327, 350, 356, 358, 362, 364, 365.

Every effort has been made to trace the copyright holders, and we apologise in advance for any unintentional omissions. We would be pleased to insert the appropriate acknowledgement in any subsequent edition of this publication.